Be Strong and Courageous

Be Strong and Courageous

Letters to My Children About Being Christian

David Yount

Sheed & Ward
Franklin, Wisconsin

As an apostolate of the Priests of the Sacred Heart, a Catholic religious congregation, the mission of Sheed & Ward is to publish books of contemporary impact and enduring merit in Catholic Christian thought and action. The books published, however, reflect the opinion of their authors and are not meant to represent the official position of the Priests of the Sacred Heart.

2000

Sheed & Ward
7373 South Lovers Lane Road
Franklin, Wisconsin 53132
1-800-266-5564

Printed in the United States of America

Cover design: Kathy Kikkert
Interior design: GrafixStudio, Inc.
Cover art used with permission: © Marco Monti-Photonica (top photograph); © Doug Pummer/Photonica (bottom photograph)

Library of Congress Cataloging-in-Publication Data

Yount, David.
Be strong and courageous : letters to my children about being Christian / David Yount.
p. cm.
Includes bibliographical references.
ISBN 1-58051-076-0 (alk. paper)
1. Christian life I. Title.

BV4501.2 .Y685 2000
248.4'82—dc21 00-041017

1 2 3 4 5 / 03 02 01 00

CONTENTS

Also by David Yount

Growing in Faith
A Guide for the Reluctant Christian

Breaking Through God's Silence
A Guide to Effective Prayer

Spiritual Simplicity
Simplify Your Life and Enrich Your Soul

Ten Thoughts to Take into Eternity
Living Wisely in the Light of the Afterlife

Dedication

To the memory of
G.K. Chesterton, C.S. Lewis, and Thomas Merton,
my own fathers in faith,
and
to the reader,
who deserves to live confidently

God orders all things with gentleness, and his way is to plant religion in the mind by argument and in the heart by grace.

Blaise Pascal

What I Wish for You

Dear Christina, Lisa, and Virginia,

Your mother and I have long since provided for you financially in our wills, but there is a more important legacy I wish to leave you. It is my religious faith. There is no way to make such a gift after one's death, so I had best make the attempt while I am still with you.

Although I write a lot about religion, I don't talk much about it, at least not in the family. Faith was taken for granted under my parents' roof, perhaps because my mother and father had the advantage of a parochial education and offered the same experience to me. You enjoyed no such benefit.

During your childhood years at home, I rationalized that I didn't want to force my faith on you. Increasingly, however, I suspect that my reticence flowed from the fact that, before you came on the scene, I not only was mismatched in the ministry but also flunked my first marriage. Until Becky married me, adopted you, and became your mother, I had my hands full as a single parent just tending to your physical needs.

You deserved better from me, and this is my tardy attempt to make amends. I fell into the common trap of equating religion with worthiness, shying from sharing my faith with you because I felt I was less a man than you (and God) deserved. In fact, religion has nothing whatsoever to do with "goodness." Consider that Jesus railed at the righteous while he socialized with sinners. The "good" people killed him. His message was that we are permanently flawed yet capable of love, which invites forgiveness.

Now you are no longer children; rather, you are adults—the same age as Jesus when he brought confidence to a people who had lost hope. On my last birthday, one of you confided in me that you no longer believe in God. Another complained that, while still clinging to faith, you no longer felt God's love. Your revelations were not the gifts I had requested to mark my passing years, but they were poignant reminders of the long years in my own early adulthood when I wandered miserably and alone in the desert of doubt.

Sunday school certainly is insufficient preparation for a life of faith. Beliefs ingested in childhood are like mother's milk: nourishing us during our infancy but inadequate to sustain adult life. Fortunately, there is such a thing as adult faith, and it is fed by solid food. God does not cease to exist when our faith in him falters. Rather, you and I exist at this very moment because God continues to believe in us. If we ceased to exist, God still would be.

Nor, Virginia, does faith rest on feeling. In his death throes, Jesus himself complained that he felt abandoned. You, alone, among your sisters have enjoyed a born-again experience, but it has not always sustained you emotionally. Do not despair.

Too much is made of the consolations of religion. God is constant in his love, but faith does not necessarily make us feel good. In fact, faith often places burdens on us that we would rather avoid. What better example than Jesus himself, who prayed to be spared torture and death only to have his Father turn him down.

At the moment, you lack confidence, not faith. In this you have plenty of company among people of goodwill who, confronting the challenges and uncertainties of adult living, discover that the faith they were fed at home and in school is inadequate for coping confidently. All Christians aspire to a childlike faith, but many of us are equipped with only a childish one. The missing ingredient is confidence, which comes from knowledge and constancy. Saint Paul, my favorite saint, puts it perfectly in his first letter to the Corinthians (13:11–13):

> *When I was a little child I talked and felt and thought like a little child. Now that I am grown-up my childish speech and feeling and thought have no further significance for me.*

Paul acknowledges the elusiveness of faith and counsels confidence:

> *At present we are looking at puzzling reflections in a mirror. The time will come when we see reality whole and face to face! At present all I know is a little fraction of the truth, but the time will come when I shall know it as fully as God now knows me!*

And then he concludes:

> *In this life we have three great lasting qualities—faith, hope and love. But the greatest of them is love.*

Rest assured, you and I do not have to wait until eternity to believe and live authentically. Faith, hope, and love are the foundations of a confident Christianity that we can begin to build upon at any time in our lives—and the earlier the better. The dour Danish philosopher Søren Kierkegäard once lamented that "life is lived forward but understood backward"—but it need not be.

Granted, Monday morning quarterbacks know the exact score after the game is over, but coaches and players understand how to play the game, which is vastly more important. So it is with life as well. Its details are unpredictable but its plan is clear. Indeed, that plan does not have to be sought out, because it has been revealed to us.

It's my experience that good people resist growing in faith for the same reasons. They plead:

If it isn't broken, don't fix it. Simple beliefs can seem reassuring even when they fail to stand up to real-life challenges. It is tempting to sequester faith in the attic of your soul as a charming fairy tale. To explore more deeply will expose you to the risk of discovering that the foundations of your personal faith are fragile, and that the truth is more often prose than it is poetry. Your faith may be as elaborate as a sand castle, yet just as vulnerable to the tides.

I'm not really religious. Few people are. At least they don't wear piety on their sleeves and make devotion an obsession. A wise bishop noted that even God has interests beyond religion. Confident Christianity is not obsessive; rather, it is informed and grounded.

I don't want to change. We all fall short of our Creator's expectations, and it's only natural to fear that the more you and I know about our faith, the more will be expected of us. If that is your surmise, you are correct. Still, any changes to your character will be gradual, and it is God who will make them—you need only cooperate. Christians are never on their own. What we achieve from a mature faith is a comprehensive perspective on life. You will begin to see things (including yourself) from God's point of view. The ordeal will become less and less onerous, because faith will have become a habit.

To some extent, every Christian nurtures excuses for failing to pursue a more confident faith. Baptized as infants (as you were) or in early adolescence, they possess a subliminal sense of membership in something significant and mysterious that they can revisit when the spirit moves them—notably when they marry, have children of their own, and approach death. Ask Americans to identify their religious faith, and nine out of ten of us respond that we are Christians. Consider the alternatives, however—to proclaim oneself an atheist? Atheism is a faith that is as impossible to prove as any other. To become a Jew, a Moslem, or a Buddhist? To do so, you would have to undergo conversion and make faith an even larger part of your life. But growing in faith is precisely what we must do to become confident Christians.

The alternative to faith is to wander through life clueless, and to die without hope. Life is fragile, and death is certain. Each of you was born with disabilities, and only you and God know how you have managed to convert weaknesses into strengths. In life you have survived the four pets who were your closest companions during childhood, and you experienced the decline and demise of your grandparents. As the poet Dylan Thomas proclaimed, "Death shall have no dominion." The confidence he expressed here can be sustained only by faith.

When I meet an adult convert to Christianity, I am always humbled and occasionally shamed. My three fathers in faith—G. K. Chesterton, C. S. Lewis, and Thomas Merton—all came late to their faith. Whereas I accept my faith as a legacy from my parents, adult converts recognize it as a gift from God, a discovery, and a revelation—the ultimate and comprehensive answer to all their aspirations and challenges, including the mysteries of life. As a young man giddy with gratitude for his existence, Chesterton searched for someone or something to be grateful *to.* Of course, it was God.

Converts embrace Christianity wholeheartedly, with humor, affection, and high expectation—and they are not disappointed. In this respect, they resemble naturalized citizens who cherish their new identity as Americans—something you and I take for granted as an accident of birth. Just as the greatest patriots are those who consider their citizenship to be a blessing, confident Christians are men and women who welcome faith as a gift that, given proper nourishment, will grow.

In every other aspect of your lives, you seek to become more effective through knowledge, because competence is the key to confidence. Faith is no exception. There is a difference, however, because faith lives in the constant company of doubt—which is no deterrent from maturing in faith, but it is cause for humility. Confident Christians are not cocksure, because they remain flawed, sinful, and even occasionally stupid. Christian confidence is constructed not from smugness but from knowledge and modesty.

You have encountered cocksure Christians on television and in the churches. Their smiling self-righteousness mocks the founder of their faith, who suffered doubt, betrayal, abandonment, and torture before he conquered death to redeem them. When Jesus spoke, he was right without being righteous. Christians are not always right in the application of their faith, so there is nothing for them to feel righteous about. We dare not pretend that God is on our side, but only hope that we are on his.

As a young man grappling with doubt and seeking confidence, I was deeply influenced by a book written by the late English theologian, Ronald Knox, entitled *Enthusiasm*. Knox decried faiths that feed on feeling, arguing that sentiment swiftly degenerates into sentimentality and cannot be sustained. A buoyant faith can outride tempestuous seas but cannot completely calm them. Confident Christians live by faith, not by emotion. They are superior to no others and are loved no more by their Creator than unbelievers—but they are better grounded in faith, more realistic in their hopes, and deeply motivated by love.

Virginia, you seek the confidence that comes from sensing God's presence, consolation, and guidance. I wish I could give it to you, but I can only comfort you with the knowledge that people through the ages have clung to their faith while praying with the psalmist:

Out of the depths I cry to you, O Lord;
O Lord, hear my voice.
Let your ears be attentive to my cry for mercy
(Psalm 130:1–2).

Like the psalmist, you recently expressed your faltering confidence in verse:

Lord, sometimes I feel so lost in this
big world you made.
When everyone else has a map,
I can't even seem to find the road.
Grown and yet a child, wise and yet a fool,
My mind and heart are full of questions
that seem to go unanswered . . .

If your heart is starved just now, then feed your mind with faith. Faith faces challenges, while skepticism seeks to evade them. It is better to hold firmly to something than to lose your grip on everything. To suspend your faith is to condemn yourself to the permanent paralysis of doubt. To be sure, Christians must often detour or retrace their steps to negotiate their way, but they have a destination to move toward. Don't malinger at the crossroads, scrutinizing and doubting every signpost—for you will get nowhere. To be without direction is to be lost.

It is far better to believe something than to doubt everything, leaving your destiny to chance. Former Yale University chaplain William Sloane Coffin affirmed that if people don't believe in something, they will fall for anything. When you make mistakes in faith and love, you can always correct them. What you can't do is *live without* faith and love.

Faith is infinitely preferable to fate. While Chesterton acknowledged that reasonable people trust their senses, he warned that only insane persons trust their senses alone. Faith is like an eyeglass, enabling you to focus your sight. Some glasses may be rose-colored or cracked, distorted or made to the wrong prescription. Proper glasses, however, help you extend your vision beyond yourselves. Telescopes extend your vision to the heavens. Without faith, you and I are prisoners of our own stream of consciousness, confined to the fickle and transient reality that resides in our heads.

Confident Christians aim to extend their knowledge beyond mere experience, and their love beyond mere mortals. Your faith, far from being superstitious, grows by testing, discarding, augmenting, and securing an understanding of the real world. With faith, your grasp will be greater than your reach. The bee sees more, the dog hears and smells more, and the snake feels more than you and I do. But the beasts' universe is infinitely smaller than yours, because you alone can transform the signals of your senses, through faith and reason, into an understanding that determines how you choose, what you value, and how you act.

Neither you nor I occupy the center of the universe; we are only a small part of it. But faith affirms that our Creator values each of us above the moon, the stars, and the galaxies. That is the foundation of our Christian confidence.

In coming to faith as an adult, C. S. Lewis exulted that he was "surprised by joy." Chesterton likened his experience to an explorer who, sailing for a distant shore, mistakenly lands on the coast of his homeland, thereby experiencing both adventure and assurance. Merton, like Augustine before him, was restless until his heart rested in God. He became a monk, then a hermit. You need be neither monk nor hermit to possess what he was given.

Early in the twentieth century, Chesterton confronted a world weary of church piety and enraptured with science and evolutionary progress. He argued that the simplicity of the saints made more sense of life than science. By the time Lewis took up his pen, science and reason had been usurped by skepticism and an aimless amorality. Accordingly, he appealed to reason, imagination, and aspiration in making his case for Christianity. Merton, brilliant but aimless in his youth, was appalled by the inhumanity of war. He made his case for Christianity from the heart.

I cannot improve on these three men as Christian apologists; their wit is as unapproachable as their wisdom. Nor has their work been eclipsed. Lewis's and Merton's books are still available in reprints, and Chesterton commands shelf space in libraries if not in bookstores. All three have long since departed this mortal coil to join their Maker. Faith, to be sure, does not play favorites with mortal beings.

You will probably be more attracted to women of faith as your models. Perhaps the high point in my life of faith was playing host to Dorothy Day when I was a college student. She was extraordinary in her faithfulness, and one day she will be recognized as the saint she is.

You may find someone like Teresa of Avila more to your liking as a model Christian. She had wit as well as her wits, was the best of friends, and was a mystic besides. Indeed, she actually met God and lived to tell the tale.

Especially in the decades since Lewis's death, fashions in thought and feeling have changed yet again. The typical American today has no argument with faith and, indeed, craves (with Merton) the hope that faith promises. But even nominal believers have lost touch with their foundations in Church and Scripture. It is as if a whole generation has forgotten the alphabet of faith—an alphabet I should have taught you in your youth. I fear that you have so small a basis for belief that there is little besides sentiment and wishful thinking for you to build upon. The case for a confident Christianity needs to be made again to meet new conditions. In these letters I hope to make up for lost time. Rest assured that what I am describing to you is the faith of our fathers and mothers, not some trendy variation on traditional themes. God lives outside time.

All this to say that there is but one God for all faiths—and for those who profess no faith. Our common Creator is neither Christian, Jewish, nor Moslem. Nor is he the product of our faith but, rather, its subject and object. We do not create God; rather, God creates and sustains us. It is a mistake to strive to find him, because he eternally reaches out to find us, in the process revealing himself and sealing a covenant with his creation. You do not even have to pray to gain his attention. You need only stop, listen, and absorb what he has told you about himself and yourselves.

Acknowledging that God is greater than any of our beliefs about him does not mean that all faiths are equally insightful, comprehensive, or useful in attaining our common destiny. Syncretism—assembling those ingredients of various faiths that please us, while discarding those that displease—treats religion like a salad bar. Religion is not an appetizer but food for a lifetime. "Designer" religions are created by persons who want to fashion easy faiths of which they, not God, occupy the center. The strength of the great world religions is that they contain accessible, comprehensive, and demanding treasures that are true to experience. The great faiths neither flinch from mystery nor treat it as esoteric wisdom. They are easy to learn and not at all easy to practice. In true religion, there is no heaven without hell, no virtue without sin, no salvation without suffering.

If there were no such faith as Christianity, I suspect that I would be drawn to another of the great religions. After all, their common subject and object is God, and the alternative to faith is hopelessness and oblivion. But Christianity is not just another faith, nor is it crafted by mortal imagination. Although it rests on the foundation of two thousand years of God's revelation to the Israelites, Christianity remains a unique and utterly unpredictable surprise. Today, yet another two millennia further along, Christianity remains as fresh and revolutionary as when the ragged John the Baptist cried in the desert, "Make straight the way of the Lord" (Mark 1:3).

To grasp how the first Christians must have felt, Chesterton asks us to pretend that we are anthropologists who come upon a tribe of people who worship a spirit who not only created them but so loves them that he sent his son to become one of them and to die to save them for an eternity of joy. Following their god's example, these hypothetical natives live in peace and are impelled by generosity, love, and high hope. Contemporary anthropologists would only judge such people to be highly civilized. But you and I would realize that theirs is the same faith that we Christians have professed all along, but applied poorly. Christianity, Chesterton argued, has not been tried and found wanting; it has been found difficult and has yet to be tried.

Believe me, every alternative to religious faith has failed. Rationalism has long since reasoned its way into skepticism. Romanticism, exalting the senses and burning the candle at both ends, produced decadence, drug dependency, and self-destruction. Science has expanded our universe only to leave people feeling small, helpless, and uncertain. Technology has given us the means to shape our environment but no clear direction or motivation.

Among recent secular faiths, fascism ended in Auschwitz; communism produced the Gulag and the Wall. Secular humanism still pretends that each one of us is the only god we need—the exact appeal the snake made to Adam and Eve in the garden. Humanism failed in Eden to account for the perversity and self-destruction in human nature. To pretend that man is the measure of all things is ultimately delusional. As for art, it uplifts the spirit but lacks the power to redeem the person. Art is an invitation to faith. So is nature but, of itself, nature is unfeeling and sometimes cruel.

Confidence in God is different from self-assurance. To believe wholly in yourself is madness; to believe in nothing beyond yourself is to embrace oblivion. Confidence comes only from your Creator, who knows you better than you know yourself, who loves you unconditionally, and who offers you a hope beyond any human expectation. Don't settle for a fickle faith. The only faith worth having is a confident faith.

When asked to characterize his own faith, the pacifist Philip Berrigan replied from prison, "I am a Catholic trying to be a Christian." All believers, regardless of denominational differences, share the same aspiration: to act like Christians. By and large, our fellow Americans manage to follow their faiths free of rancor or intolerance. Our very diversity of religious expression—as many as a thousand distinct Christian denominations—does not weaken the faith we hold in common; rather, our diversity seems to strengthen our faith.

In *Mere Christianity,* C. S. Lewis argued that the central theme of our faith is vastly more important than any denominational variation on that theme. Rest assured, your growth in confidence will make you a more effective Christian whatever church family you choose to join.

I write to you, my children, at the turn of the millennium, the significance of which rests wholly on the appearance of Jesus of Nazareth two thousand years ago. Ever since, the world has reckoned time as if it began with Jesus' birth. Two millennia later, the faith he founded claims the allegiance of 1.6 billion men, women, and children—one-third of the world's population—who believe themselves blessed with great expectations. The faith you share with them is founded on Good News as fresh and relevant as it was when Jesus delivered it from the hills of Galilee. God willing, you will live long into the third Christian millennium. I pray that you will live it confident in your faith, your hope, and your love.

Faithfully,

Your father

Part I

Faith

Faith is the substance of things hoped for,
the evidence of things not seen.

—Hebrews 11:1

CHAPTER 1

Make Friends with Jesus

What are we to make of Jesus Christ?
This is a question which has, in a sense,
a frantically comic side. For the real question
is not what we are to make of Christ,
but what is He to make of us?

—C. S. Lewis

Dear Christina, Lisa, and Virginia,

Christianity is all about what Christ has done for you, me, and everyone. You owe it to him—and to yourselves—to learn more about this extraordinary person who is your best friend.

For us Christians, time had two beginnings: originally, when our Creator completed his task of love and pronounced it "good."

> *So God created man in his own image,*
> *in the image of God he created him;*
> *male and female he created them*
> (Genesis 1:27).

That was the first time. We have no idea how long ago it happened, but shortly thereafter something went seriously wrong with God's creatures. They damaged themselves and needed mending.

The second beginning of time occurred two thousand years ago, when a child like no other before or since was born to redeem creation and make it good again. This person was not only made in the Creator's image (as you are) but was God's own Son. Christians and non-Christians alike measure time from that moment. Moreover, all previous time is counted backwards from his birth, as if in anticipation of it.

With the appearance of Jesus, eternity was injected into time. Although our senses fail to reveal it, everything about life since that defining moment has changed—and we have been mended. Jesus grew into manhood, preaching, healing, forgiving, suffering, dying, and conquering death at no one's behest but his Father's. In the process, he accomplished for you and me what we cannot manage on our own: saving us from ourselves and redeeming us for an eternity with God. Jesus founded a permanent Kingdom of God on earth, no less real for being invisible, because you will discover its reality within your hearts and souls.

Jesus' promise was that, as creatures of love, you and I are henceforth invulnerable to decay and the ravages of time, destined to return to the Creator-Father whose image we bear. To guide you toward that common destiny, God's own Spirit resides in your bodies and souls, ensuring that when you pray and align your wills with his, it is God himself who animates you.

As a visible resource, Jesus created the Church for your instruction, mutual support, and common worship, and as an instrument of grace. Virginia, you worked as receptionist for a large church, and I suspect you found the work little different from other office jobs you have held. Nevertheless, you sense that the Church is not a building or a corporation; it is God's family of which we are members.

This is the faith common to all Christians; this is also the glory we share. It is not for sale, for it has already been purchased for us at a harrowing price—the death of God's Son. It is, quite simply, a gift. Let us make friends with the giver.

A Revolutionary Faith

Lisa, you are an accomplished artist. Since your childhood, you have seen so many idealized portraits of Jesus that you may think you know him. In fact, even those closest to Jesus in his lifetime possessed scant understanding of who he was and what he was accomplishing. It was only after his death and resurrection that the Christian faith took root and flowered in human comprehension. Nevertheless, even as Jesus addressed the crowds during his brief ministry, his message, although imperfectly understood, turned the world upside down, shattering every complacent preconception of what is to be honored, valued, and expected in life.

At the time of Jesus, the Roman-dominated world was at peace but worshiped war. In that political atmosphere, Jesus preached that those who take up the sword will perish by it. He blessed not warriors but peacemakers. Addressing his society—the majority of whose members were impoverished, enslaved, and despised—he blessed the poor, promising that God's kingdom is their rightful inheritance. You can't pass a homeless man or woman on the street without knowing that God loves that person as much as he loves you. Jesus counted slave equal to master and woman equal to man in God's sight, and cautioned that it is easier for a camel to pass through the eye of a needle than for the rich and powerful to inherit the kingdom.

Jesus railed against righteousness and mere law-abiding, setting love and compassion in their place. To the self-righteous moralizers who plagued him, Jesus prescribed repentance and conversion, and he forgave sins. Against popular opinion, he insisted that illness and disability were not punishments for moral fault. Then he healed the sick and cured the lame, the crippled, and the blind. Death, Jesus insisted, has no dominion, and to prove it, he raised the dead to life—finally, by the sacrifice of his own life, conquering death for all eternity.

Although you will die one day, you will never stop living—because of Jesus.

There was no one like him in history, before or since, who practiced precisely what he preached. He insisted on utter, radical democracy, in which everyone made in God's image enjoys the same privileges, prospects, and respect. The privileged establishment, however, hated him for his insistence on equality, and executed him. But, over time, people loved him for it, and his faith and the hope it contained spread like wildfire. Within three centuries after his death, Christianity was the faith of the empire. Again, today, it is the faith of one-third of the world's people.

Jesus is unique among religious leaders. Mohammed claimed only to be a prophet, the Buddha to have tasted enlightenment, Abraham to be God's servant. Jesus alone professed to be God's Son. Let's examine his claim.

Jesus the Mythmaker

According to his critics, Jesus' most lasting fault was that he never gave an account of himself but left it to others to tell us about him. They charge that the reporters—principally the Evangelists and St. Paul—created a mythical God-man from a small-time country preacher.

They are correct in this respect alone: the Gospels are not journalistic reports or transcripts of history. More than mere chronicles of an outspoken Jewish preacher who met an untimely death, they are testimonies of faith that this man holds the key not only to history but to eternity. So, are the gospel accounts false to Jesus because their authors had an agenda? Did they make Jesus into something he never was and never intended to be?

Before attempting to answer these questions, ask yourselves this: If Jesus had written his own story instead of relying on others to tell it, would his critics have believed him? Not likely. You know from your own reading that people who write their own memoirs tend to flatter themselves. For their real-life stories, we do better to read biographies written after their death.

What critics of religion decry is that Jesus did not expose himself to them directly. Sending Jesus to his death, Pilate was frustrated because his prisoner refused to defend himself or answer the Roman's cynical question: "What is truth?" (John 18:38). As you recall, Pilate didn't want to hear Jesus' truth because it would have made demands on him.

If, for the sake of argument, we allege that the New Testament authors merely created a myth about Jesus, they must, at least, have believed it themselves, because they devoted their lives to proclaiming their faith, enduring hardships, and suffering persecution. Most of them, in fact, were imprisoned and executed for their beliefs. How likely do you think it is that men so simple and so fickle in Jesus' presence would become so sophisticated and courageous after his death, proclaiming a myth of their own creation that would sway billions of people and shape subsequent history? If Christianity is a myth, it is of Jesus' own making, not the contrivance of his friends.

The Truth behind Myths

What do you imagine a myth is? Don't be too quick to dismiss myths as fairy tales, like those I read to you when you were young. Rather, a myth is a truth that is neither literal nor necessarily figurative. As adults, we believe in many myths; we believe in honor and patriotism, motherhood, happy endings, love and enchantment. Christians do not confess that they *believe* Jesus, but that they believe *in* him. To believe is merely to acknowledge; you have reason to believe there is something called gravity, for example, but you don't have to think much about it. To believe *in* someone is to embrace that person, acknowledging not just that person's words, but the person himself. Jesus' friends found him to be not only credible but indispensable—the key that unlocked their souls and their destinies, and made sense of living, loving, and dying.

As you are well aware from our absences, Becky and I are Anglophiles, and we visit Britain whenever we can. Were I to ask an Englishman if his country is the land of Arthur and Camelot, he would laugh at me—politely, of course. But he could not dismiss the signs and monuments of his nation's monarchs and the glory and spirit that dominate his cities and countryside. Is a castle or cathedral less real because it is ancient? No, it is real, and myth is the significance that resides in its silent stones. Religious critics may carp that English churches today are largely empty of believers, but they cannot dismiss the fact that the Church is still there.

Myth is what one makes of things, but it is rooted in reality rather than in imagination. One does not make a myth of oneself. You would frown on an otherwise virtuous mother who constantly reminded her children of her generosity to them. We honor our own mothers, however numerous or limited their virtues, because it is important to believe in motherhood. Similarly, we respect the person who occupies the White House—whether or not we voted for him—because we believe in the presidency.

So it is with religion, where faith overshadows knowledge. When preachers pose the perennial question, "What do you think of Jesus?" they demand that you not just acknowledge him but that you make a judgment about him. Just as in heaven there are many mansions (see John 14:2), there are as many relationships to Christ as there are persons who love him. Superficially, the Jesus of St. John's Gospel contrasts with the Jesus of St. Paul's letters. But Jesus is the same; only the writers' appreciation differs. (In life, the apostle John was physically embraced by the Lord, whereas Paul fell to the ground, blinded by a Jesus he had never met in life.)

If, as journalists, the Evangelists neglected to tell us the vital statistics of the historical Jesus, it is because they recognized that his age, height, complexion, build, and tone of voice were beside the point—the point being that he was the Christ and that he is our first, last, and only hope. Had Jesus left us his memoirs, we might have risked losing the Jesus of myth, who is Lord. Critics would have dismissed him as yet another preacher out to justify himself. Instead, he left no record other than the faith of his followers and the legacy of his conquest of death.

If Jesus did not create his own myth, then, how true is the myth to the man?

Who Tells Us about Jesus?

Anyone approaching the New Testament for the first time would assume that the four eyewitness accounts of Jesus' life—the Gospels—predate St. Paul's letters, which serve to explain the significance of his life. It is only natural to expect to read the story before the explanation of the story—or, in modern parlance, the message before the myth. But that was not the case. The first of Paul's surviving letters dates from within fifteen years of Jesus' death, whereas the first gospel account to be set down (Mark's) was written anywhere from fifteen to twenty-five years afterwards, and the last accepted account (John) was written quite late in the first century.

The explanation of the story unpredictably preceded the writing of the story. How can that be? The only plausible explanation is that eyewitness accounts of Jesus and his teaching were the subject of storytelling long before they were set down formally in writing. Because Paul's missionary territory extended throughout the empire, he was unable to keep in touch by voice and was required to write letters—not unlike these letters I'm writing to the three of you.

Moreover, it is not surprising that Paul himself did not fancy that he was a gospel writer. He was the least qualified candidate, because he was chosen as an apostle only *after* Jesus' life, death, and resurrection. Although he was a witness to the risen Christ, Paul never knew Jesus in the flesh—but he knew the story, as other first-generation Christians did, from the preaching of eyewitnesses. Paul turned his handicap into a virtue by grasping and explaining the *meaning* of Jesus.

The New Testament must be read as a piece to make sense of Christianity. The Gospels, for example, relate what Jesus said and did during his brief ministry; the epistles of Paul and others explain Jesus' timeless significance for Jews and Gentiles alike. No Christian of the first century waited for a gospel to be written before making a commitment to Christ; rather, the earliest Christians had listened to the story often enough to grasp its meaning for their lives. The Acts of the Apostles is a history of that preaching that covers roughly the years A.D. 30 to 60. Revealingly, Luke wrote it at about the same time he wrote his Gospel, instead of long afterwards, as you might anticipate. He recognized that Jesus' life and the proclamation of its meaning were all of one piece.

As a journalist myself, I find it extraordinary that we have few accounts of Jesus' life by disinterested reporters. Then again, Galilee and Judea were not exactly plum assignments for foreign correspondents of the time. No newsmen and newswomen followed Jesus around to record his every utterance the way the White House press corps tags along with the president today. Only those few persons who truly cared about Jesus chose to remember what he said and did. And when, many years later, a few of them produced written records, they wrote not new bulletins or histories but testimonials of faith.

Today, two thousand years later, critics of Christianity still carp that the Gospels do not meet contemporary journalistic standards in describing the historical Jesus—the who, what, when, where, and why of him. If someone asked one of you to write a description of me, I'd be surprised if it read like a police report. I would not be surprised if you wrote about me as your father, because that's my relationship to you. In that same fashion, the Evangelists did nothing to hide the bias of their faith in Jesus; nevertheless, their accounts are strikingly straightforward and free of manipulation. The Gospels are anything but public-relations puff pieces. They are gritty stories of pain, disappointment, betrayal, and triumph. The Evangelists set down what mattered to them about Jesus—the Jesus they knew and believed in, who had changed their lives forever, who can change yours and mine today.

Jesus, the Obscure

How do you explain the fact that the most important person in history was so little acknowledged in his own time? His humble beginnings surely had something to do with it. Jesus was the son of an obscure carpenter from a provincial village in a tiny defeated nation. At the age of thirty, he began a brief public life, but he wrote nothing that has survived, held no office, and spoke from no public platform. In fact, he never left his homeland. No one bothered to note his appearance for posterity. He spoke to no more than a few thousand people during his ministry, most of them ordinary country folk, many of whom dismissed him. At the first sign of trouble, even his friends fled; no one lifted a finger to save him. Within three years, still a young man, he was dead—executed as a common criminal.

Do you sometimes think that Jesus would have been more persuasive had he chosen a different time and place to enter history? Nowadays, of course, no television evangelist could survive preaching to audiences as small (and poor) as Jesus' were. But what if Jesus himself occupied their pulpits right now and enjoyed the freedom of the airwaves and communications satellites to speak simultaneously to millions if not billions of people?

I believe that you would be disappointed. After all, what could Jesus say now that he neglected to say then? And if he merely repeated his two-thousand-year-old message, he would only offend a contemporary audience with his warnings against ambition, wealth, lust, and hypocrisy. It would be interesting to have Jesus address contemporary world problems, of course, but it is notable that he chose not to address similar issues when he spoke two thousand years ago from the hills of Palestine. For example, he did not condemn slavery, he bid soldiers only to be dutiful, and he merely acknowledged everyone's requirement to pay taxes.

In short, Jesus did not lecture the politicians of his own time, and it is unlikely that he would change the thrust of his message today. He was not politically correct; indeed, Jesus was not political at all. You have heard people argue that, as a social reformer, Jesus was an impractical dreamer. But he did not aspire to improve society. Rather, his message was personal, timeless, and universal. He called for repentance, conversion, hope, and love, founding a kingdom not of this world nor, for that matter, for any particular time or place. It is the ultimate irony that a man with so little interest in government was executed by politicians as an enemy of the people.

Revealingly, Jesus said nothing to Christians—for the simple reason that there weren't any Christians during his lifetime. Rather, he spoke to his fellow Israelites as their brother. Your faith as Christians today did not spring full-blown from Jesus, but from a long legacy of God's revelation to the race from which Jesus sprang. If Jesus was an obscure figure in first-century Palestine, so was his race, but it was uniquely blessed and prepared for his appearance. Had he entered history at another time and in some other place, the entire burden of God's revelation would have been on Jesus' shoulders. Fortunately, in his three brief years of preaching, Jesus enjoyed the distinct advantage of being able to refer to what his countrymen and countrywomen already knew and to the God they already worshiped.

In the end, Jesus was rejected by his own people, but Christianity has never rejected Judaism; it merely built upon its base and universalized the old revelation, prompting Pope Pius XI to say that you and I and all Christians ought to regard ourselves as "spiritual Semites." After all, the Bible Jesus taught from was the Old Testament, originally given to his fellow Jews and which we Christians have inherited whole. Jesus himself embodies the New Testament.

Who Was He?

The great theologian Adolph von Harnack acknowledged that all we know about Jesus from sources other than the New Testament can be summarized on one small sheet of paper. Thus, you are required to meet Jesus through the testimony of his friends.

At the outset of their Gospels, John and Matthew introduce Jesus to us from different points of view. John's Jesus, for example, is the eternal Son of God born of the heavens. He writes:

> *At the beginning God expressed himself. That personal expression was with God and was God, and he existed with God from the beginning . . . He came into the world—the world he had created—and the world failed to recognize him* (John 1:1–2, 10).

Contrastingly, Matthew introduces Jesus by tracing his purely human Jewish ancestry back to the patriarch Abraham and to King David. Matthew begins:

> *This is the record of the ancestry of Jesus Christ who was the descendent of both David and Abraham.*

Then he lists a bewildering number of names of fathers and sons, finally naming Joseph, "the husband of Mary, the mother of Jesus Christ," and concludes:

> *The genealogy of Jesus Christ may thus be traced for fourteen generations from Abraham to David, fourteen from David to the deportation to Babylon, and fourteen more from the deportation to Christ himself* (Matthew 1:1–2, 17).

Because Matthew was writing to persuade Jewish readers, he introduces Jesus as the long-awaited Messiah whose mission was to save Israel. John, writing much later for mostly non-Jewish Christians scattered across the empire, introduces Jesus as not only an exalted human being, but the very model after which the world was patterned:

> *All creation took place through him, and nothing happened without him* (John 1:3).

We Christians regard Jesus to be at once God and man, and have tussled with that apparent contradiction for two thousand years. Jesus preferred to refer to himself as Son of Man but, when pressed by Pilate, he acknowledged that he was also the Son of God. No matter: he was rejected by his own people on both counts and sent to his death by the Romans. Jesus' miracles were neither grand nor numerous enough to convince either religious leaders or politicians of his divinity, and the human figure he cut as a provincial preacher failed to impress an indifferent nation.

In yet another contrast, the Evangelist Luke introduces us to Jesus as an infant in what we know as the Christmas story: the babe of Bethlehem born in a manger. Signaling his identity, a star leads the Gentile kings to honor him, while angels announce him to the Jewish shepherds.

Taking yet another tack, the Evangelist Mark introduces us at the outset of his Gospel to the adult Jesus, identified by his cousin, John the Baptist, as "the one who is to come" (Mark 1:7).

What Was He Like?

Generations of Christians like yourselves have become accustomed to a cardboard Christ—impeccably robed and haloed, with a permanently placid expression on his handsome face. It is as if, by conceiving of Jesus as a perfect man, the artists hoped to make him appear divine. In fact, the gospel accounts depict a Jesus who was not at all serene but tired, hungry, sleep-deprived, angry, disappointed, passionate, fearful, tempted, demanding—and sometimes seemingly indifferent. (And we can be confident that Jesus didn't bathe as often as you and I do and that he didn't send his clothes to the cleaners.)

Christina, you are a social worker, treating seriously troubled people, some with destructive fantasies. Imagine dealing with a client who was simultaneously divine and human! If that combination didn't qualify Jesus as schizophrenic, it certainly explains his unpredictability. How else might we interpret the episode in which the parents of the boy Jesus, fearing he was lost, searched frantically for three days, only to find him in the Temple disputing with teachers? Whereupon, rather than calming his mother's distress and asking his parents' forgiveness, Jesus chided them by saying: "But why were you looking for me? Did you not know that I must be in my Father's house?" (Luke 2:49).

If one of you had pulled such a stunt on your mother and me at that age, you would have been grounded! But Jesus' Mother, although hurt and confused, chose only to "treasure all these things in her heart" (Luke 2:19). Before all others, she knew her child to be someone special.

We cannot fathom what went on in Jesus' head and heart except perhaps during those poignant moments when he prayed aloud to his Father in fear and longing, and when he wept. Nor have we any notion what he looked like. Can this be because he did not cut an impressive figure, or did the Evangelists simply consider it pointless to describe the human features of God?

Much of what we know about Jesus' contemporaries comes from statues, friezes, and wall paintings that depict pagan gods and prominent persons. Lisa, you studied these likenesses in art school, and you know that most renderings are idealized. Despite the medieval mania for collecting purported relics of the cross on which he died or the garments he wore, no Christian presumes to have a notion of Jesus' actual appearance. Even if the Shroud of Turin is proven to be the authentic burial cloth in which Jesus was buried, it offers few clues. In the Roman catacombs, Jesus is depicted as clean-shaven; later artists, however, were persuaded that by giving him a beard, Jesus would look more distinguished.

Our modern idealization of Jesus can be traced to a forged document of the early sixteenth century, which masqueraded as having been written by Publius Lentulus, successor to Pontius Pilate as Roman governor of Judea. In his work *Jesus, Man of Joy*, Sherwood Wirt tells us that, according to the forger:

> *He is a tall man, well shaped and of an amiable and reverend aspect; his hair is a color that can hardly be matched, falling into graceful curls . . . parted on the crown of his head, running as a stream to the front after the fashion of the Nazarites; his forehead high, large and imposing; his cheeks without spot or wrinkle, beautiful with a lovely red; his nose and mouth formed with exquisite symmetry; his beard, and of a color suitable to his hair,*

> *reaching below his chin and parted in the middle like a fork; his eyes bright blue, clear and serene.*

Contemporary theologian Philip Yancey, however, points to a legend dating from the second century that suggests Jesus may have been a hunchback. In medieval times it was widely believed that he was a leper. Isaiah predicted this of the Messiah:

> *Just as there were many who were appalled at him—his appearance was so disfigured beyond that of any man and his form marred beyond human likeness . . . He had no beauty or majesty to attract us to him, nothing in his appearance that we should desire him. He was despised and rejected by men, a man of sorrows, and familiar with suffering. Like one from whom men hide their faces he was despised, and we esteemed him not* (52:14; 53:2–3).

This "man of sorrows" surely suited God's purposes better than a serene Hollywood-style Jesus. Except during a single episode (the Transfiguration), the Gospels depict Jesus appearance as unexceptional. John the Baptist, in fact, confessed that he would not have recognized Jesus as anyone special were it not for a special revelation.

His Character

If Jesus' appearance was unremarkable, what do you imagine accounted for his sway over people? His apostles, you will recall, did not choose him; rather, he chose them, and they immediately dropped everything—including work and family—to follow him. According to author Philip Yancey, in his work titled *The Jesus I Never Knew*, the emperor Napoleon, no pious zealot, said this of Jesus:

> *Everything in Christ astonishes me. His spirit overawes me, and his will confounds me. Between him and whoever else in the world, there is no possible term of comparison. He is truly a being by himself . . . I search in vain in history to find the similar to Jesus Christ, or anything which can approach the gospel. Neither history, nor humanity, nor the ages, nor nature, offer me anything with which I am able to compare it or to explain it. Here everything is extraordinary.*

It is reassuring to think of Jesus as calm and collected, but the Gospels indicate he was anything but. For example, he was emotional; one moment he was "filled with pity" and the next he was "moved with compassion" (Matthew 9:36) and on occasions he wept in front of his followers (see Luke 19:41; John 11:35). Unlike cardboard heroes, Jesus did not hide his fears or fail to ask for help. "My heart is nearly breaking," he told his apostles on the night before his execution. "Stay here and keep watch with me," he pleaded in his solitude (Matthew 26:38). But as you recollect, his friends failed to take his anxiety seriously and dozed until he was arrested and taken from them.

Philip Yancey remarks of Jesus that "he had nearly inexhaustible patience with individuals but no patience at all with institutions and injustice." Depending on the circumstances, Jesus expressed compassion, grief, disappointment, or anger. Rather than draw attention to his own powers, it was characteristic of Jesus to compliment the *recipients* of his miracles: "Your faith has saved you" (Matthew 9:22). He was the most intimate of men; people immediately warmed to him, and strangers revealed their hearts to him. Philip Yancey cites novelist Mary Gordon as calling Jesus the most affectionate hero in all literature.

For the most part, Jesus avoided the sophisticated society of the cities, preferring to preach to the provincials from whom he sprang. He undoubtedly spoke in Aramaic, rather than Hebrew, and with a country accent, was considered uneducated by the learned. Yet, the Gospels reveal that Jesus spoke with such command that crowds sat for three straight days without food, just to hear him. Even those long-winded twentieth-century despots, Hitler and Castro, couldn't command crowd attention for more than a few hours.

Dietrich Bonhoeffer, the German theologian martyred by the Nazis, admired Jesus' ability to be "the man for others." Characteristically, at the wedding reception of friends, Jesus worked his first miracle for no more profound reason than to save the couple from embarrassment, because the wine was running low. Jesus was never the show-off, preferring that those he cured make mention of the fact to no one. He accepted anyone's invitation to dinner, proving himself friend of the mighty and the miserable, the rich and the poor, foreigners, soldiers, prostitutes, tax collectors, the halt, the lame, the blind, and the lepers.

But C. S. Lewis, in his work titled *The Four Loves*, warns that we should not thereby conceive of Jesus as a populist. "You can't really be very well 'adjusted' to your world," he said, " if it says you 'have a devil' and ends by nailing you up naked to a stake of wood."

His Inner Life

It is probably presumptuous—and pointless—for you and me to attempt probing Jesus' inner life. But if he is to be our friend, we will naturally aspire to understand what he thought and how he felt. How describe the state of mind and soul of a God-man except to acknowledge that, as God, he felt constrained by his humanity and, as man, endured the constant pressure of his divinity? That Jesus handled this permanent tension without succumbing to neurosis, collapse, or delusions of grandeur is a measure of the strength of his character. I'm certain, Christina, that you would like your clients to be so well-balanced.

Unlike prodigies who set about to display their genius, Jesus had nothing to gain from asserting his divinity. He sought and gained neither fame nor fortune, and died a convicted criminal. Even as a helpless infant, Jesus was the Son of God, first-born of creation, and the model for all humanity. In his divine nature, he must have been constantly tempted to break through his humanity and dependency. At the outset of his ministry, retreating into the desert to strengthen himself for his mission, Jesus was enticed by Satan to assert pride and seek comfort which, as God, he had every right to demand. Revealingly, he rejected the grandeur of divinity in favor of wrestling with human temptation because it was as man that he would offer his life to save his friends—including you and me.

I don't want to put you on the spot, but the only way you can deny Jesus' claim to divinity is to characterize him as a madman or a liar. The Gospels offer no supporting evidence of self-delusion or misrepresentation. Jesus was neither fool nor braggart. The Gospels do suggest, however, that the human Jesus did not bear his burden of divinity lightly. Rather, he must have constantly struggled to reconcile himself to who he was and what he was destined to do. When Jesus prayed to his Father, he reached out—not within himself—for guidance and conviction. Here was a divine being who experienced hunger and thirst, anxiety, exhaustion, treachery, disappointment, sorrow, and hatred—the human condition. And yet, far from floating above trouble, he confronted it. In the face of his fate, he did not despair. Death became his deliverance—and ours.

Virginia, you have appeared on the stage. You know that even brilliant actors with confidence in their roles and lines can suffer stage fright. Jesus doubted neither himself nor his Father, but he certainly experienced fear. The divine Jesus who calmed a storm that threatened to drown his friends was also the human Jesus who had to be wakened by them from his exhaustion rather than be drowned in the boat with them. When his time finally ran out, Jesus prayed to his Father for a reprieve, which was denied, submitted to torture and humiliation, and went to his death with these words on his lips: "My God, my God, why did you forsake me?" (Mark 15:34).

Jesus' Credibility

In subsequent letters, I will ask you to consider whether what Jesus said and did—his preaching, forgiveness, miracles, resurrection, and promise of eternal happiness—are credible. For now, I hope you will find him trustworthy, not as an actor or mouthpiece but as a person and a friend. You will trust what he said and did only if you trust him.

Today, some of your contemporaries deny that the Holocaust ever happened and consider moon-walking to be an elaborate hoax. So, too, there are those who not only do not believe in Jesus, but who consider him to be a figment of our overheated imaginations. It is true that Jesus failed to attract the attention of the chroniclers and historians of his time; then again, few written records of any sort survive from the first century. It seems logical to assume that Pilate, a bureaucrat, would have routinely reported Jesus' trial and execution to his superiors in Rome, but no records whatsoever remain from Pilate or, indeed, from any other Roman governor of Judea. We are thrown back on the testimony of Jesus' friends.

The prevailing lack of interest in Jesus among non-Christians of his own century is illustrated by Luke in his

Acts of the Apostles. He quotes the offhanded remarks of the politician Festus, about the Jews and St. Paul: "They simply had some points of disagreement with (me) about their own religion and about a certain dead man, Jesus, whom Paul asserted to be alive" (Acts 25:19).

Except for a contested quotation by the Jewish historian Flavius Josephus (born A.D. 37), collateral evidence for the life of Jesus does not appear until the second century. It is clear, however, that there were Christians from the outset. The existence and explosive growth of his church is the most telling evidence for Jesus.

What Jesus Accomplished

He came to reconcile all humankind to its Creator and to offer eternal life to those who love God: that is what confident Christians believe to be Jesus' purpose.

Of course, not everyone agrees that he succeeded. But look around you and see how life has changed for the better because of him. Granted, people are still flawed, but no one believes today's world to be the same brutish, enslaved, superstitious tyranny that it was when Jesus came to save it. Because of Jesus' influence and the faith of his followers, the world is, if not yet the New Jerusalem, certainly a much better place.

Because Jesus insisted on the equality of all men and women, we have long since insisted on equal treatment before the law. Because Jesus praised the Good Samaritan, benevolence and generosity are now prized over cruelty and indifference. Because Jesus chose peace over war, no Christian nation takes to arms lightly. Because Jesus was unafraid of the truth and despised superstition, we promote literacy and education. Because Jesus held life sacred and cured the sick, so do we.

Jesus believed there was no such thing as a *common* man or a *common* woman; rather, he believed that every human creature is extraordinary. Grasping that belief, peoples have fought for personal freedom, civil rights, and democracy. Because Jesus urged forgiveness over punishment, he appealed to the best in human nature, and we have gradually graduated from barbarism to civilization. Because Jesus praised the poor and the weak, wealth and power are no longer virtues, but only gifts. Because Jesus' life inspired art, music, and literature, all of us are richer for it. Because Jesus forgave faults, you and I can acknowledge ours and change for the better. Because Jesus was the Good Shepherd, none of us will be lost. Because Jesus overcame fear, we can find confidence.

These are the legacies of Jesus that every person inherits at birth, whether or not they believe in him. But faith is his greatest legacy, and reaps the ultimate reward. Faith is ever available, and I hope you will embrace it wholeheartedly. All it requires of you is to say "yes" when Jesus invites you to follow him.

Dreams and Joy

G. K. Chesterton, raised to consider Jesus a cardboard caricature, was shocked as an adult to discover that the real Jesus in the Gospels was:

> *. . . an extraordinary being with lips of thunder and acts of lurid decision, flinging down tables, casting out devils, passing with the wild secrecy of the wind from mountain isolation to a sort of dreadful demagogy; a being who often acted like an angry god—and always like a god.*

Ultimately, Jesus is a mystery to us, because there has never been another person like him in whom humanity and divinity coexisted in peace. But it is impossible not to speculate about his inner life or to be attracted to him as a friend.

Do you ever wonder what this strange God-man dreamed about? God, of course, never sleeps, and has no need of fantasy. He is the ultimate realist; all creation is the product of his imagination. But what of Jesus the man, an exhausted wanderer, often with only a stone for a pillow and the stars for a roof over his head?

I suspect that, in his dreams, Jesus discovered a peace in his dual identity that eluded him in his waking life, renewing the intimacy between the human and the divine that had been lost after Paradise. His entire brief ministry, after all, was aimed at recapturing that very intimacy for you and me—that inner Eden.

I suspect, too, that Jesus often smiled in his sleep. Awake, he never hid his tears or his anger, his pity or his compassion; and at the end, he did not hide his fears. But alone at prayer, or asleep and dreaming, he was free to feel what Chesterton and Lewis call the gigantic secret of every confident Christian. That secret is joy, and it is what I wish for you.

Faithfully,

Your father

Chapter 2

Listen to God

Jesus did not say
"Go into the world and tell the world that it is quite right."
The Gospel is something completely different.
In fact, it is directly opposed to the world.

—C. S. Lewis

Dear Christina, Lisa, and Virginia,

Where shall we go to gain confidence? Some Christians prefer to go directly to God in prayer, seeking instruction and solutions; but that is a privileged and solitary path, and the option of last resort. Prayer is a fundamental part of Christian life, but those who resort to it only in desperation will be inclined to accept just the answers they wish to hear. Had God chosen to reveal himself exclusively through personal messages to us, there would be no need for Scripture or the Church, and Jesus need not have made his terrible sacrifice for us.

It is clear that God does not choose to operate by personal revelation, so we must gain confidence by other means. He prefers to deal with peoples corporately, and with individuals only as messengers and leaders. Christians don't wait by the phone expecting God's call. For confidence, we turn to what all of us possess in common: the Bible and the Church.

The Secret

Asked by a visiting African chief to reveal the formula for her successful sixty-seven-year reign over the British Empire, Queen Victoria presented him with a Bible, declaring, "Here is the secret!"

Three centuries earlier, the great Protestant reformer Martin Luther had preempted the monarch's claim, arguing that it is impossible "to rule a country, let alone the entire world, by the gospel. God has placed human civil life under the dominion of natural reason, which has the ability to rule physical things. We need not look to scripture for advice."

Who was wiser, do you think: the queen or the churchman? For Christians like ourselves who seek personal confidence, the answer is of little consequence. The fate of nations is not in our hands. What we do seek is counsel on how to lead responsible, fulfilling lives—caring for those entrusted to us and trusting God to keep his promises. To give Victoria her due, the queen was persuaded that personal virtue was the secret to a happy life for herself; for this, she found the Bible a source of strength and inspiration. It helped her to be a better person.

The Bible can be a source of strength for you as well. But the challenge you will encounter at the outset is that the Bible is formidable in length—my copy runs to 1,862 pages of tiny type—and, to all appearances, lacks any coherent plot. Its text is complex, often arcane, and is filled with apparent contradictions. Dictionaries and encyclopedias are alphabetized for easy reference, but we need a weighty concordance to find our way in the Bible. Is it any wonder that people desperate for inspiration open the Bible at random and blindly lay their finger on a verse hoping it will impart the wisdom that will show them the way? I've been tempted to do that myself. Unfortunately, the Bible does not lend itself to use as a ouija board.

Those who manage to read the Bible from cover to cover, beginning with Genesis, are like the weary adventurers who hike the length of the Appalachian Trail. They remember only the highlights of the journey. The rest is mindless drudgery.

Lamentably, Scripture is often employed as a weapon. Christians who oppose each other on public issues such as abortion, animal rights, homosexuality, capital punishment, and euthanasia, for example, often quote passages from the Bible to justify their positions. No surprises here: it has long been conceded that the devil himself can quote Scripture to his advantage. There is so much in the Bible that it is easily quoted out of context and twisted to give the wrong signals.

Have I utterly discouraged you? I hope not. We probably demand too much of written revelation. The Bible was never intended to convey a comprehensive set of solutions to life's problems. In the final analysis, you must think for yourselves. Consider this: if we relied only on the *letter* of Scripture, we might still tolerate slavery, and women would be second-class citizens. Luther surely had a point: conscience and reason are also our guides. When in doubt over what to do, compassion is always a good rule of thumb.

For all the Bible's complexity, Moses managed to compress God's commandments to ten, and Jesus further reduced them to two: to love God and to love our fellow creatures. In his Sermon on the Mount (see Matthew 5–7), Jesus added refinements to those commandments which, at first blush, confuse rather than clarify what God expects of us. Jesus exalted poverty—a condition every sensible person abhors—then transformed sorrow, suffering, and meekness from vices into virtues. Moreover, he instructed us to love our enemies and pray for those who treat us badly.

On encountering these precepts, you can be forgiven for not finding them to be clear formulas for confident living; they seem to make Christianity more of a burden than a consolation. Still, this is how God chose to speak with us, so let us persist.

Extracting Treasure

Despite its apparent drawbacks, every generation has been drawn to the Bible as to a vast mine that contains treasure, undeterred by the fact that some of the gold is difficult to extract. And every generation has preached the Bible, in season and out. When you were young, we read to you from Robert Louis Stevenson's *A Child's Garden of Verse.* At the tender age of three, the author, on learning that sheep and horses knew nothing about God, asked his nurse to read the Bible to them for their salvation.

As a child myself growing up in the Church, I was taught to memorize those Bible verses that tended to support positions my denomination itself took and to disregard others. Consequently, by early adulthood, I was knowledgeable *about* the Bible—but I was far from Bible literate. My shortcomings were never so apparent as when I began the ordeal of promoting my first book through radio call-in shows around the country, many of them on Christian stations. My callers were courteous with their questions, but many were clearly better equipped than I to summon Bible chapters and verses at will from memory to trip me up. Even when my interlocutors' understanding of the Bible was inferior to their rote memorization, their facility was a humbling revelation, and I determined that henceforth I would develop a deeper familiarity with the written word of God.

Fortunately, biblical studies have developed such sophistication during the past century that Jewish and Christian scholars of widely divergent traditions now enjoy many more points of agreement than disagreement. With the occasional assistance of experts on obscure points, you can be the wiser, enjoying the confidence that comes from submitting your challenges and aspirations to God's written word.

Having said that, I also admit the difficulties you will encounter. Unlike other best-selling books, the Bible is read only selectively, not cover to cover. The churches wisely mete out critical selections over the course of a year so that worshipers receive a representative smattering of revelation that roughly summarizes their faith. Consequently, the sermons you hear from Sunday to Sunday tend to be based on relatively few passages. I have heard preachers, for example, devote an hour to dissecting a single phrase! That practice, far from depriving us of the Bible's wisdom, aims to make sense of it.

Another challenge: the Bible piles genealogy upon genealogy, belaboring some tales for pages and dismissing others in a paragraph. It casually leaps over entire centuries and is mostly vague about time. Indeed, if you take its account of creation literally, the Bible blithely disregards countless millennia between Genesis and Exodus, its first two books. Biblical authors, most of them anonymous, mix fact with legend, and morals with myth, with perfectly good intentions but to our occasional befuddlement. In taking on the Bible, you had best begin at the beginning but, after examining the first two books, you may find better understanding by proceeding selectively.

The Hollywood Bible

When you were in school, you had *Cliff's Notes* as shortcuts to understanding the classics. Well, the Bible has Hollywood as its popular teacher. Although it is touted as an uplifting document, the Bible proffers a cast of heroes and villains suited for wide-screen melodrama. The Bible's evil characters operate on the most primitive motives of lust, envy, greed, and blood-thirst—and its heroes are, if anything, constructed of thinner cardboard. They are either self-righteous, blindly compliant, or as violent as their enemies in meting out justice. Some are devious, others cowardly. Like their villainous opposites, they are flawed, only in lesser measure. Often their only claim to heroism is that they listen to God and obey him.

For sheer story value and characterization, the Bible received its best reading from Cecil B. DeMille and his imitators, who fixed on sin and slavery, exotic casts of thousands, special effects, and great disasters to flesh out Old Testament tales of piety. As a young person, my most vivid recollections of the Bible were of Charlton Heston as Moses parting the Red Sea, and Victor Mature as Samson bringing down the Temple. At will I can replay in my mind's eye the scene in which the Israelites, enslaved in Egypt, are employed to erect the pyramids. While hauling the great stone blocks in teams, a slave slips and is crushed beneath the future monument to the pharaoh. Grisly stuff, the Bible!

Your Sunday school classes opted for sanitized versions of many of the same stories. Instead of fixing on Sodom and Gomorrah, for example, you read heroic tales of Joseph abandoned by his brothers, of Noah enduring catcalls for building a boat in the desert, of David felling great Goliath with a stone, and of Daniel taming hungry lions. With these and a few other exceptions, the heroes and heroines of the Bible, by and large, tend to be poor candidates for engaging your imaginations as children, let alone stirring your nascent faith. A Sunday school teacher would look askance at a child who wanted to grow up to be like Jeremiah or Isaiah.

Considering its drawbacks, what could possibly account for the massive sales of a book so tedious in length, meandering in plot, quaint in expression, and short on heroism?

A Book Like No Other

Judaism and Christianity, whose book the Bible is, do not apologize for it. In fact, it is their pride and their foundation—the one reference all believers agree on. Granting the Bible's apparent shortcomings as literature, they insist that it is a book not meant for light vacation reading. Like the Yellow Pages, Standard & Poors, Valueline, and Roget's *Thesaurus,* the Bible is a specialized reference. That the Bible proved accessible on any level to moviemakers is astounding. It is a tribute to the vast audiences of believers and aspirants to faith who found in film an entry into the complex world of the Bible.

The Bible is a compendium of God's dealing with his people, initially those who formed the tiny, fragile nations of Israel and Judea—then expanding to include peoples of all nations, including you and me. Strictly speaking, therefore, biblical revelation is not the story of individuals. If some characters in the Bible appear to be thinly drawn heroes and villains, it is because they enter the story only to illustrate a point or to act as a vehicle for God, who is the Bible's only real hero. Some characters are legendary; indeed, some biblical critics consider them *only* legendary. Their role in the Old Testament is to illustrate the story of God entering history to heal the breach between creatures and Creator. In the New Testament, God enters history in the person of his Son. Having initially created man in his image, God now makes himself in man's image.

An arresting story has compelling characters and a tight, fast-paced plot. The Bible, by contrast, tracks God's many dealings with a whole people over long centuries. That may make for a meandering story—but it also makes for a reliable God. Because of God's faithfulness, the Christian can find confidence in his revelation.

Studying the Bible

Bible study has been facilitated in recent years by the personal computer, which can scan for word, subject, and phrase. At a recent book fair in London, your mother and I witnessed bearded young Orthodox Jews at computer keyboards calling up God's revelation on-screen with just a few educated taps of their fingers. Computer gurus inform us that the word *and* occurs in the Bible 46,227 times and the word "girl" appears only once. The shortest verse is John 11:35: "Jesus wept."

For Bible hobbyists, it is tempting to become involved in such trivial pursuits. But the Bible itself is anything but trivial; it is God's own word. Every now and then, a publisher produces the Bible in a version meant to be read not as revelation but as literature. Such versions are tightly condensed and selective to keep them interesting and undemanding. By contrast, the real Bible is often tedious but always insistent. It is a book meant to be not just *read* but *followed*.

Not surprisingly, the Bible is the world's best-known and most-published book. Its contents have long since been translated into nearly a thousand different languages and dialects. Even thirty years ago, the British and Foreign Bible Society alone was printing one copy every three seconds around the clock, night and day, seven days a week, just to satisfy demand.

The word "Bible" comes from the Greek word *biblia*, which simply means "books." The Bible we know is a single book only in the sense that it collects many books between its covers. The Old Testament, of course, is the Bible Jesus knew and used. It consists of thirty-nine separate books. Lamentably, none of the original handwritten manuscripts has survived, the first of which were made about fourteen hundred years before the birth of Jesus and recopied by hand as the originals deteriorated. Whereas other ancient peoples carved in permanent stone, the Jews wrote on perishable scrolls. Then again, they had a lot to record.

Until 1947, our oldest available copies of the Hebrew Old Testament dated from only the ninth or tenth century *after* Christ. Then, in the caves of Qumran near the Dead Sea, Arab shepherds discovered copies of the Old Testament that actually antedated Jesus by more than a century. Comparing them with later copies, scholars discovered—to their delight—that the texts we use today are remarkably faithful to the originals. Not that this was a complete surprise: to ensure accuracy, biblical scribes routinely counted all the words and letters of the originals, matching them to their copies.

Books of the Old Testament

The thirty-nine books in the Old Testament comprise three kinds of literature: seventeen histories (Genesis to Esther), five poetical books (Job to Song of Solomon), and seventeen prophetical works. Additional Hebrew holy texts, known collectively as the *Apocrypha*, were accorded equal respect in the early Greek translation (285–246 B.C.) known as the *Septuagint*. These writings were included in the original King James version of the Bible and are still honored as biblical by Roman Catholics.

For ease of study and reference, the Bible is now arranged for us in chapters and verses—a convenience not found in the original books. Stephen Langton, Archbishop of Canterbury (d. 1228), first divided the Bible's books into chapters. More than four centuries later, Robert Stephanus provided the now-familiar verse numbers.

Originally, the Bible was copied onto scrolls of parchment, vellum, or papyrus, some of them extending up to forty feet. Late in the first Christian century, an attempt was made to sew individual pages into what we now call a book. This kind of "packaging" provided a more convenient format for reading and a more economical product, because copyists could write on both sides of the page.

The lengthy Old Testament was compiled over more than a thousand years, as God revealed himself progressively in his creation, then to Noah, Abraham and his family, Moses, David, and generations of Jews. In comparison, the New Testament is relatively brief and was composed in a matter of decades after the death of Jesus. This quick and compact production probably stemmed from the Christian conviction that, in Jesus, God had made his final and complete revelation. The Bible now had a conclusion; after Jesus, there simply was nothing more to add.

Books of the New Testament

The New Testament consists of twenty-seven books: the four familiar Gospels; plus letters of Paul, Peter, James and Jude; Luke's history of the early church (Acts), and the Book of Revelation (or Apocalypse). All were written in Greek. Fragments of the New Testament text remain from as early as the second century, and there are as many as fifteen thousand complete manuscripts and fragments available to scholars for comparison to ensure the accuracy of our New Testament today.

The authors of the New Testament clearly had no intention of writing a "new testament." The written Gospels, for example, were afterthoughts, preserving the oral accounts of Jesus' life provided by eyewitnesses. Scholars assume that the Evangelists made use of a written compilation of Jesus' "sayings," but that document, if it ever existed, is lost. The letters are just what they seem—instructions intended for specific readers. Their practicality is their value.

It is clear that the first generations of Christians expected the world to end during their lifetimes. They could not have conceived of anyone—like the three of you two thousand years later—wanting to know Jesus' story. That fact alone probably accounts for the random way the books were written and, much later, collected and hallowed. They read like journalism rather than literature.

Understand that the New Testament was not imposed on the Church; rather, it was chosen by the Church as an integral part of its life and worship. The earliest Christians simply read from the Hebrew Bible that Jesus preached from. We do know, however, that by A.D. 200 the Church was already making official use of the four

Gospels and Paul's letters. The remaining books were more slowly accepted, while many competing books were rejected as fanciful and inconsistent with oral tradition.

Every few years, publishers "discover" a new gospel they believe unlocks some divine mystery heretofore hidden from us. There is nothing novel about such writings; fake accounts were a dime a dozen in the early Christian world and were rejected by the Church. Every few years, for example, someone rediscovers "The Gospel of Thomas," an account composed in the second century but judged to be fanciful. Notably, it was not until the fourth century that the entire Church agreed on the contents of the New Testament—forty-two years *after* it had agreed on the Christian creed! Remarkably, it was the same man, St. Athanasius, who crafted the creed and successfully argued for the books that deserved to be included in the New Testament. The Church clearly serves not only as the custodian of Scripture but, in this sense, as its source.

Versions of the Bible

Because of modern printing, the Bible is accessible to anyone who can read. Unlike other books, however, it is seldom read in its original languages—Greek and Hebrew—but in vernacular translations. There are eight different English "versions" of the Bible on my bookshelf, each of which expresses God's revelation in a slightly different voice and nuance. When I quote the New Testament in these letters, I use the translation by the late English scholar J. B. Phillips. What his version occasionally loses in poetic expression, it gains in clarity and common speech. Here, for example, is how Phillips presents a portion of St. Paul's famous discourse on love in 1 Corinthians 13:

> *This love of which I speak is slow to lose patience—it looks for a way of being constructive. It is not possessive: it is neither anxious to*

> *impress nor does it cherish inflated ideas of its own importance.*
>
> *Love has good manners and does not pursue selfish advantage. It is not touchy. It does not keep account of evil or gloat over the wickedness of other people. On the contrary, it is glad with all good men when truth prevails.*
>
> *Love knows no limit to its endurance, no end to its trust, no fading of its hope; it can outlast anything. It is, in fact, the one thing that still stands when all else has fallen.*

Phillips takes 117 words to translate verses 4–8. By contrast, the widely used New International version expresses the same thoughts in only sixty-one words:

> *Love is patient, love is kind. It does not envy, it does not boast, it is not proud. It is not rude, it is not self-seeking, it is not easily angered, it keeps no record of wrongs. Love does not delight in evil but rejoices with the truth. It always protects, always trusts, always hopes, always perseveres.*
>
> *Love never fails.*

And the hallowed King James version makes do with only half as many words:

> *Charity suffereth long and is kind; charity envieth not; charity vaunteth not itself, is not puffed up, doth not behave itself unseemly, seeketh not her own, is not easily provoked, thinketh no evil; rejoiceth not in inquiry, but rejoiceth in the truth; beareth all things, believeth all things, hopeth all things, endureth all things.*
>
> *Charity never faileth.*

Do not be bewildered that the identical message can be expressed so differently in the same "foreign" language—English. In a sense, the original Greek New Testament was itself a translation of Jesus' revelation, because he spoke in neither of the biblical languages, but rather in Aramaic!

Confidence in the Bible

On occasion, confident Christians are challenged by skeptics to vouch for the truth of the Bible. If you are so prodded, be wary: it is an unfair demand. Truth may be stranger than fiction, but novels are often truer to life than journalism. The Bible is composed of narratives, stories, letters, songs, poetry, and prophesy. As you know, no one demands that a song or a poem be historically accurate, but only that it reflect true sentiment. Nor do you demand that tales be historically verifiable, but only that they have an authentic moral purpose and their characters ring true. Happily, the Bible is often true in the former sense, but it is *always* true in the latter: its contents always have an authentic moral purpose. That is why it is a great book that claims our attention.

During my career as a journalist, I routinely reported facts accurately but occasionally got the story wrong. That is, my details were factual, but they led me to a conclusion that missed the real point of the story—and it is the story that counts. As you know, newspaper tradition forbids reporters the luxury of writing their own headlines; another person at the paper does that, expressing in a very few words what the reporters' stories mean. Just so, the human authors of the Bible were inspired by God to write their reports of his revelation, but God provided—and continues to provide—the meaning. It is, after all, his story.

Some Christian apologists attempt to defend the accuracy of every detail in the Bible, reckoning that God is in the details. Their efforts are noble and surprisingly successful, but ultimately marginal. The Bible's individual books were written at different times for different purposes and different audiences; moreover, the authors' intentions were rarely literal or scientific.

When you were young, your mother and I did not drag down a dictionary, encyclopedia, or book of fairy tales to teach you good behavior. Instead, we attempted to teach you by example and sometimes by punishment. Similarly, the Bible is filled with instances of God teaching lessons to his childish people, not by recitation but by action—floods, swarms of locusts, political defeat, and exile. God is not just a talker; he is also a doer.

Fortunately, where the Bible's meaning is obscure, scholars can help lift the veil on its mysteries for you. Most contemporary Bibles include interpretive notes. In the last analysis, however, the Bible is not your task to verify and defend, but God's story to tell. Strictly speaking, your faith as confident Christians is placed not in the Bible itself but in its ultimate Author and your personal Creator: God.

How Jesus Used the Bible

It is tempting to treat the Bible as an icon—a portable object of faith that you can hold in the palm of your hand. The president of the United States takes his oath of office with his hand resting on the Scriptures. Christianity is known as a "religion of the book," because it claims the Bible as a fixed reference for its faith. But that advantage can be overstated.

Now that you are living on your own and must prepare your own meals, you no doubt often rely on cookbooks. I like to think that the Bible comprises Christianity in much the same manner that a cookbook claims to contain all the meals in its recipes. But just as hungry persons cannot be satisfied with a cookbook alone, confident Christians will not be satisfied by just reading the Bible. Cooks and Christians must turn what they read into reality.

To use another metaphor, a book of maps points the way but will not actually convey you to your destination. Confident Christians are guided by faith, inspired by hope, and driven by love to their destination, which is God himself. The Bible, in fact, constantly warns of the dangers of idolatry—of worshiping something or someone more convenient, more tangible, or less demanding than God. It is tempting for some Christians to idolize the Bible itself and to seek justification in its pages for their own biases. It has long been noted that Satan himself can quote Scripture for his own purposes. He did so when he tempted Jesus in the desert (see Mark 1:12–13).

But Jesus lived by the Bible; he did not write it. He quoted from it and assured his listeners that he had come to fulfill what he quoted. When challenged by his critics, he typically countered, "But have you not read . . . ?" (Matthew 12:3) referring to the Bible as the authority that stood behind what he had to say. His clear message was that his critics had misread or distorted God's revelation. To end an argument, Jesus would proclaim: "It is written . . . " and explain the true meaning of Scripture (Luke 22:37).

What was written in the Old Testament was the extraordinary chronicle of God's acts of creation and the on-again, off-again love affair with the creatures he intended to be most like himself—men like me and women like you. Not that God himself was fickle in his affections, but his love for humankind was routinely unrequited. The Bible can be read as proof of humankind's perversity—a chronicle of all-too-human attempts to go it alone without our Creator and Sustainer. That is its tragic plot line. But the Bible is more usefully read as the story of God's faithfulness against faithlessness—the Creator's determination to save his creatures from themselves.

Although the Deity in the Old Testament is often depicted as an angry God, any unbiased reader of the Bible must conclude that he had every right to be exasperated with humankind's treason. Again and again, God is provoked and he punishes, but he never writes off humankind as a failed experiment.

At the outset, God reveals himself as the unique and sole Deity, competing with no other gods for human attention. There are, of course, no other gods. Moreover, he reveals himself to be Creator rather than craftsman—a concept utterly foreign to the pagan mind, which conceived only of gods who could manipulate and destroy but not create. Instead, God reveals himself to have created the universe from nothing and for no other motive than love.

The Creature Made to Love

In his ultimate act of exuberant affection, God creates a thinking, feeling animal who has the capacity to forge a personal relationship with the Creator. Although it is, of necessity, a dependent relationship from the human side, this ultimate creature, nevertheless, bears the likeness of the Creator himself. Awarded dominion over the rest of creation, men and women choose to rebel against their Creator, deluding themselves that free will gives them independence from God.

Before moving on in the Bible story, you should note that God created the world out of *nothing,* not as an appendage of himself. The perennial temptation of philosophers and theologians is to discover God wholly within his material creation, such that everything from wine barrels to slugs to babies is an aspect of the divine. In the Bible, God clearly reveals that he stands apart from his creation, but not aloof from it. Poetically speaking, it may be true that there is God in every creature, but we are not gods. Christians believe that God's Spirit resides in each person as a gift, but we are not thereby transformed into God. From dust we come, and to dust we will return.

The Old Testament testifies to the fact that the special creatures God made in his own image could not wait to assert their independence from him. In theological terms, this presumption is known as original sin. The very first pair were ejected from their earthly paradise precisely because they aspired to an autonomy for which they were ill-equipped by their Creator—to be gods themselves.

The first humans were ejected from the garden for their presumption, but they were not rejected by their Creator. Nevertheless, human perversity escalated, as the couple's son murders his brother out of envy. In time, God sends a flood to devastate all but Noah and his family, and humankind makes a second start with a new pact with its Creator, marked with the sign of the rainbow. Still, human beings continue to exceed their grasp, as a new generation seeks to storm heaven by constructing a tower (the Tower of Babel) tall enough to reach God, who frustrates their design by confusing their speech—which is where we get the term to *babble*.

If these early biblical accounts appear fanciful to you, they are, nonetheless, compelling stories with a clear moral—which is their point. If you tell me a joke and I fail to laugh, there are three explanations: either it was a poor joke, it was poorly told, or I didn't get the point. If I am required to ask you to explain the joke, it's doubly guaranteed that I won't laugh even when I do grasp it. Analysis is the enemy of humor.

So it is with tales in the Bible, but in these instances we *do* get their point, because they are effective stories. No one bothers to analyze a gag after it produces a laugh, but people of a skeptical bent are prone to dismiss biblical stories as mythical even when they have grasped the storyteller's point and admit it contains wisdom. The *point* of the story of the Tower of Babel, for example, is that creatures presumed to co-opt the Creator and failed. To accept the story as inspired does not require you to believe that God at that instant created all the world's languages to confuse them.

Truth and Fancy

The reformer Martin Luther was well aware that critics, by analyzing the Bible down to little pieces, often miss the point altogether. "Reason," he said, "is the greatest enemy that faith has: it never comes to the aid of spiritual things but—more frequently than not—struggles against the divine word, treating with contempt all that emanates from God."

Jesus chose to continue the biblical penchant for revealing God's truth through stories. It is clear that his characters—the Good Shepherd, the Good Samaritan, the Prodigal Son, the Sower, the Owner of the Vineyard, and others—are products of the storyteller's art. Jesus is not a journalist reporting on individuals with names, addresses, and telephone numbers, but a teacher with a gift for creating vivid characters whose stories persuade our minds, touch our hearts, and change our lives forever.

C. S. Lewis was sympathetic with scholars who maintain that the biblical accounts of creation and the flood are probably derived from ancient Semitic stories that were mythical in origin. But Lewis balked at the notion that the biblical accounts can be thereby reduced to pagan fancy. Rather, he noted that the original tales had been developed, corrected, and reworked into accounts that describe a transcendent Creator and a true creation. In short, the old myths had been altered to serve God's purposes; they became inspired. When you were young, you read Lewis's own stories which, though fanciful, conveyed truth better than the daily newspaper.

Some eighteen centuries before Jesus' birth, God reentered history to chose a nomad, Abraham, to be the father of a chosen people. By no measure was Abraham a conventional hero. He was often evasive, defensive, reluctant, and even cowardly. But at critical moments, he proved to be responsive and faithful—something his descendants routinely failed to be. One need not look far in the Old Testament, however, to discover that its true hero is God himself.

The biblical story of God's faithfulness continues with Moses, David, and the prophets—with the enslavement of the chosen people, their freedom, followed by exile, homecoming, defeat, and foreign occupation. Some four centuries before Jesus' birth, the Bible stops—pauses, perhaps—in its revelation, as if in anticipation of him. The Old Testament ends with the expectation that God will send someone to save his people from themselves.

The Search for the Historical Jesus

Modern biblical scholars, not content to merely explain the Bible, attempt to cut away its layers of myth, poetry, and revelation to discover its underlying history. They are particularly keen to discover the historical Jesus, as opposed to the Jesus of faith whom you love.

Theirs is not an unworthy search, but it is ultimately doomed, because the Bible is a testament of faith, not of history. Pilate and the Pharisees knew the historical Jesus and did not believe his claims, but they took him seriously as a threat and had him executed. Had Pilate written an account of Jesus, it would not be more credible than the Gospels, because he failed to take Jesus seriously. Pilate demanded of Jesus, "What is 'truth'?" in ignorance of the truth himself (John 18:38). The merely historical Jesus, if he could be found, would be the subject of skepticism, not faith. The Gospels are calls for you to believe in him.

The Jesus preached by the televangelists is often a caricature of the Jesus we find in the Bible. To correct the preachers' facile distortions, you must seek the Lord in the Gospels. Even then you will find him elusive, because his teaching cannot be grasped by the mind alone. As C. S. Lewis attests, "He hardly ever gave a straight answer to a straight question." Instead, Jesus preached by proverb, paradox, hyperbole, irony, and parable. As a consequence, it is not easy to assent to what he said; we must assent to *him*. He did not plead, "Listen to what I say;" rather, he commanded, "Follow *me*," and "Learn of *me*." I hope you will.

The Gospels are good news—*your* good news. They are neither biography, history, nor propaganda, but testimonials of faith calling for faith. In approaching the Bible for study, we can't pretend to start from zero-based objectivity. We approach with belief, curiosity, or skepticism. Even the most doubting persons who open the pages of the Bible today are the unwitting products of a Christian culture, now two thousand years old, ingrained in the way they think and the things they value. Even our literature and law bear the indelible mark of faith.

Reading the Bible

It is customary in American hotels, grand and humble alike, for a Bible to be provided in every room. They are placed there not by management but by a group of Christian businessmen and businesswomen, the Gideons, who know firsthand the loneliness of the traveler far from home. The Gideons have no denominational axe to grind, only a conviction that this book literally serves as a life preserver. At the end of a day in a strange place with no one to talk to, a traveler is prone to long thoughts, and they are not always life-sustaining.

The Gideons recognize that a Bible in an impersonal hotel room can be a very personal thing. In endpapers to their edition, they attempt to make the Bible speak to the needs of the man or woman who picks it up. "Are you discouraged?" "Have you suffered loss?" "Are you feeling alone?" "Are you confused?" they ask. They then refer the traveler to a Bible verse or story that responds to that emotion. The Gideons intend the Bible to be read in brief passages for consolation and inspiration, but the end papers also summarize the major revelations contained in the Bible—the stories of creation, the fall from grace, and redemption in Christ. The Gideons know that travelers don't have a lot of time on their hands, so they provide a simple map.

A path is needed through the Bible, because it is both easy and hard to read. Easy because its language is so straightforward; difficult because the book is such a jumble of seemingly unrelated bits of literature—poetry and song, letters, sermons, narratives, histories, allegories, and genealogies. The Bible is like an attic—full of precious old things no one wants to throw away but doesn't need readily at hand. There are treasures to be found in the biblical attic, and some things that can afford to gather dust. How to find what you need?

Rule 1

Do not start at the beginning as you would any other book, working your way through to the end. The Bible has a basic plot but, if you just plunge in, you will have trouble discerning it; you will find yourself diverted here and there as you proceed from book to book as in a maze.

Rule 2

Don't start at the end to see how the story comes out. The last book of the Bible, Revelation, is the hardest of all to understand, and it may also scare the wits out of you. Remember the Four Horsemen of the Apocalypse? They are part of the cast of Revelation, and they may disincline you to delve further.

Rule 3

Don't study the Bible as though it held secrets or is subtle. There is plenty in the Bible that is unclear, but many things may have been unclear to the authors as well. Besides, the Bible doesn't try to answer all questions that interest you. The Bible is right for the ages, but each book was written for specific purposes in the past and deals immediately with that time and audience, not ours. Don't instantly demand of a passage: "What is God telling me here?" Determine first what he was telling the people at the time, then see how your situation may be similar.

Rule 4

Don't expect science or literalism or perfect consistency. The Bible contains revelation, not laboratory research. We know more about the physical world than the Bible's authors did, but that does not make us right and them wrong. Look for the moral. It is good for all time, for the wise and the simple alike. Complex truths are, of themselves, no better than simple truths. Indeed, simple truths tend to humble us and clear our minds and wills.

Rule 5

Don't be put off by the chapter and verse numbers. These road signs were imposed on the ancient text in modern times to help people locate passages. That is their only function.

Rule 6

Don't expect to be inspired by the characters in the Bible. I know that Sunday school likes to make heroes of key characters, but even the protagonists lapse into jealousy, cruelty, greed, cowardice, and worse. Think of Abraham who passed off his wife as his sister, and Peter, who denied that he even knew Jesus. One of the reasons the Bible is so persuasive is that its cast of characters is so true to life, which is to say full of contradiction. But these flawed characters become heroic when, presented with hard decisions, they choose to obey God's command.

Rule 7

Do not be put off by the miraculous. See wonders as signs of God's interest and intervention. You may prefer natural explanations of the flood, the parting of the Red Sea, and Jesus' healing the sick. What is important is to see God's hand in it. The miraculous is a sign that God cares. Not that God is a "mister fix-it," stepping in to patch up every problem. Our problems are our responsibility.

Rule 8

If you think of the Bible as a vast supermarket, you are not far wrong. But you can shop for the wrong things and come up with a bad diet. Remember: the devil can quote Scripture to his benefit. Generations of Jews and Christians have cited portions of the Bible as justification for their outrageous behavior. Deny the temptation to cite the Bible to support your own prejudices and rationalizations. Resist in enrolling God in your righteousness. Instead, seek God's wisdom and God's will.

Rule 9

Reading and quoting the Bible is no substitute for acting on what God reveals there. The two great commandments are to love God and to love your neighbor. All the rest is footnote.

Rule 10

Read with others, who will protect you from eccentricity. Remember: the Church created the Bible, and it is in the Church that you will gain perspective on God's revelation, which speaks to us corporately, not individually.

Good reading! Good news!

Faithfully,

Your father

CHAPTER 3

Join the Family

When the world goes wrong,
it proves that the Church is right.
The Church is justified,
not because her children do not sin,
but because they do.

—G. K. Chesterton

Dear Christina, Lisa, and Virginia,

Here is a story you have heard before, but not from this angle.

Christianity was already more than a millennium old, suffering from the long Dark Ages and exhausted from its quixotic Crusades, when a young Italian soldier found himself at a crossroads in his life. Francesco Bernardone was accustomed to praying for guidance in the ruins of the Church of St. Damian, a neglected shrine in Assisi. Agonized by indecision whether to abandon his military career when he could conceive of no respectable alternative, the young man heard a voice say: "Francis, don't you see that my house is in ruins? Restore it for me."

With the touching simplicity that would adorn the rest of his life, the young Francis of Assisi accepted God's command literally and set about to restore the shrine, stone by stone, to its former glory. To finance the restoration, he not only impoverished himself, but made his father an unwilling collaborator by confiscating and selling bales of the elder Bernardone's cloth, piously marking them with the cross.

Infuriated, Francis's father imprisoned his son as a common thief until he was repaid in full. Then, undeterred, Francis did more: "Not only the money but everything that can be called his I will restore to my father," he said, "even the very clothes he has given me"—which he proceeded to shred into rags. Then, clothed in rags himself, he announced: "Until now I have called Pietro Bernardone father, but now I am the servant of God."

Now there's an instance of "tough love" that backfired. (Imagine casting one's own child into prison!) Still, there's a better point to this true story.

The Stone the Builders Rejected

In Matthew 7:9, we hear Jesus asking the crowds that followed him, "If any of you were asked by his son for bread, would you be likely to give him a stone?" Ironically, Francis's father gave his son *neither* bread nor stones. Undeterred, with no money and only his bare hands to continue the work, Francis scoured Assisi, begging stones from citizens to rebuild their church. To humor the pious eccentric, the townspeople gave him more than enough to complete the job. But he would beg food for the rest of his life, just as a homeless person does today.

Of course, we realize that Francis in his simplicity had mistaken the meaning of the voice. God did not intend him to be a do-it-yourself contractor, restoring houses of worship, any more than Jesus, by designating Simon as "Peter—the Rock," meant the apostle to be his Church's physical foundation. The Church that Peter led and Francis renewed is made of something other than stone.

In 1302, Pope Boniface VIII proclaimed there to be no salvation outside the Church. That sounds arrogant and narrow-minded, especially when you consider that the pontiff meant the Roman Catholic Church alone. But he had a point, and it is this: the Church exists for our salvation. That is its job. Christians are not solitary pilgrims; rather, we have one another. The Church is but a vast extended family, with God as our Father, Jesus as our Brother, and God's Spirit as our Counselor. Since we all have the same inheritance, it's imperative that we join the family.

Confident Christians acknowledge that the faith we follow is neither a philosophy nor an ideology, neither a personal possession to be guarded and cherished nor an exclusive club membership that allows us to mingle with our coreligionists. God purposely revealed himself to the *community*, first to the Jews and then to the Gentiles, rather than to select individuals. Accordingly, you cannot be a solitary Christian nor a mere Bible Christian. You must worship in common and serve others who seek to follow Jesus. That family is the Church.

Jesus ensured us that "where two or three people come together in my name, I am there, right among them!" (Matthew 18:20). Unfortunately, as we move into the third Christian millennium, it has become difficult to distinguish the forest of faith from its trees—to appreciate the one family of Christ when all we see are different churches. Despite appearances, it was this common Church that Jesus had in mind when he called Peter to lead it, Francis to restore it, and the rest of us to serve it.

The Infant Church

It's hard to imagine a time when there weren't churches on every street corner. But even today, when a church family is being formed, its members temporarily hold services in homes, schools, and even outdoors. In his Acts of the Apostles, the Evangelist Luke depicts a time when there were believers but no church buildings.

Christianity was a missionary movement, with the apostles establishing small communities of believers in the cities of the Roman Empire. Predictably, the early Christians kept a low profile rather than attract suspicion and enmity, so there was no rush to construct church buildings. Because the apostles continued to be faithful Jews as well as Christians, they appealed initially to the resident Jewish community, using the local synagogue.

Although the apostles' efforts were not always well received, the synagogues were the logical places to start before moving on to public forums. Happily, the ancient world was surprisingly literate and loved to debate philosophy and religion. Listening to a preacher—and heckling him—was almost a public entertainment in the cities of the empire. Remember, this was before television!

As small groups of local believers were formed, they met weekly in homes to reenact the Lord's Supper and to nourish themselves by reading the Old Testament and recalling the eyewitness accounts of Jesus' life, death, and resurrection. They prayed together, supported one another, and shared their possessions in the expectation of the immanent return of their Lord in glory. Those Christians in Jerusalem continued to worship in the Temple. Because the apostles were compelled to move on and carry the gospel to new towns and cities, each resident community had to develop its own leaders; nevertheless, the apostles kept in touch by letter.

Of the letters known to us in the New Testament, by far the greater number are attributed to St. Paul. Distinctive about all these communications, regardless of their author, is the fact that they serve a function distinct from the Gospels. Unlike the Gospels, they do not tell us what Jesus did and said; rather, they told the local congregations of the time the *meaning* of Jesus and how they must function to be the one Church of Christ.

You would assume that these early communities were ruled by the gospel; but the Gospels as "books" had not yet been written! Instead, the churches were inspired by the living eyewitnesses of Jesus' life, death, and resurrection; and they were guided by the apostles' letters. Paul's earliest letters to the churches were composed fifteen years *before* the first written gospel account.

Unlike other charismatic leaders, Jesus did not create an exclusive organization during his lifetime to carry out his work after he passed from the scene. Instead, he chose twelve apostles to symbolize his contemporary mission to the twelve tribes of Israel. With them, he maintained his fidelity to Judaism and his credibility as a Jew. At the time, Jesus' disciples were known only as one of a number of sects claiming to be the "true Israel." In this regard, the Nazarenes had plenty of competition from the Pharisees, Sadducees, Zealots, and Essenes, among others.

It was only after Jesus' death and resurrection that the Church actually came into being, consisting of men and women who joined in faith in the Resurrection, the expectation of the Kingdom of God, and the return of Jesus. At the outset, church members were known as the "saints," the "elect," and the "community of God"—and Christianity was known as "the Way." But from the start, Jewish Christians were distinguished from their fellow religionists by the stress they laid on baptism, the Lord's Prayer, the Lord's Supper, hope in the Resurrection, and service to one another. They were distinctive in yet another way: they loved one another. Even their antagonists marveled at their display of mutual affection and caring. Love was the glue that held the church family together.

How I do go on in these letters! (You can always skip over the dull parts.) But perhaps you will be interested to know that the New Testament's term for "church" is pagan and political in origin. *Ecclesia* originally referred to an assembly of citizens who have been summoned by an official. To this day, the Romance languages use variations of this Greek word to identify the sacred gathering of believers. "Church" in French is *eglise*. By contrast, our English word, *church*, comes from Byzantium by way of Germany and means "belonging to the Lord." To belong to the Church is to belong to Christ.

The Church and the Kingdom

Unlike yourselves, the earliest Christians lived in imminent expectation of the consummation of history, when Jesus would return to usher in the Kingdom of God. They thought heaven was right around the corner, and this expectation accounted for their fervor. Clearly, their hope was not fulfilled in their lifetimes—nor as yet two thousand years later. Nevertheless, the earliest Christians remained confident, and so do we.

From time to time, pious Christians have attempted to reconcile the delay by pretending that the Church itself is the kingdom. French theologian Alfred Loisy was not being cynical when he wrote that "Jesus proclaimed the kingdom of God, and what we got was the church." Loisy meant only praise for the Church, but it is apparent that the Church, however animated by God's Spirit, is not the consummation that you and I await.

Christians wait, while others demand paradise now. For example, international Communism established oppressive political regimes as interim arrangements that would eventually dissolve, yielding a utopian "dictatorship of the proletariat"—a kind of heaven on earth. It never happened.

By contrast, the Church proclaimed—from the outset—the permanent reality of the reign of Christ. The Resurrection was the sign that his reign has begun, and that reign continues two thousand years later. Nevertheless, it is not the consummation, and we still pray together: "Thy kingdom come . . . " as a matter of future hope and eager anticipation.

As long as Christianity was a sect with Jerusalem as its home base, the Church was tied to its Jewish roots. But two early developments won the Church its freedom. The first took place in A.D. 49 and has since been labeled the *Council of Jerusalem*. Only several years after Jesus' death and resurrection, the apostles gathered to make a momentous decision: whether gentile converts to

Christianity were to be required to convert to Jewish practices as well. The prevailing notion was that converts must submit to painful circumcision and agree to arcane dietary and other restrictions. Paul, himself a Jew, argued that one could be a Christian without being a convert to Judaism. Single-handedly, he won his argument with the original apostles, with one concession to them—that the gentile churches would financially help support the church in Jerusalem.

The last impediment to church growth was removed in A.D. 70, when the Romans destroyed Jerusalem after putting down an insurrection. Because the local Christians were pacifists and refused to join in the fight, they were branded traitors by the conquered Jews and were forced to flee the city. Jerusalem was lost as the center of the new faith, and the Christian split with Judaism became irreparable. After only one more decade, all serious attempts to convert the Jews to the new faith were abandoned. Oddly enough, that failure freed the Church to conquer the world. No longer pitted against Judaism, it soon became a threat to Rome. Persecution produced solidarity and further defined the Church as the extended family of the crucified Christ.

Little more than three centuries after the birth of Jesus, the empire itself became Christian. By this time, the Church's center was in Rome, and it was sufficiently organized to protect itself against the civil authority. Whereas the infant church had consisted of extended families of Christians holding property in common, the institutionalized Church now became a vast source of social welfare.

As a social worker yourself, Christina, you can appreciate how expensive it can be for a community to serve the poor. Well, the Church had plenty of money because it inherited the estates of Christians who feared that their personal wealth could exclude them from salvation. They took literally Jesus' warning that it is easier for a camel to pass through the eye of a needle than for a rich person to enter heaven (see Matthew 19:24). As Rome itself came under attack from the barbarians, and the capital of the empire was moved to Constantinople, the Church was the only institution powerful enough to preserve the social order.

From the outset, however, the Church had a more important role: to preserve the purity of the Christian faith.

Safeguarding the Faith

The more you examine Jesus' teachings and promises, the more confident you will become of him and of yourself. You grow in faith by relying on Jesus; but it cannot be a mere emotional attachment. The daily demands of living require faithful people to think as well as to feel, and to make decisions based on their best knowledge.

Which is only to acknowledge that your Christian faith is more than spiritual sentimentality. Religion tells you how things *are* and what you must *do* to conform to reality. It does not tell you how you must *feel*. In every age there are people who would prefer religion to be purely inspirational rather than dogmatic and moral. But just as one cannot base an entire marriage on a single love song, confident Christians cannot sustain their faith with sentiment alone. In the last analysis, of course, Christianity provides the ultimate consolation: eternity with your God. But the way to eternity is often bereft of comfort, and Christians are sustained more by what they believe than by how they feel.

From the outset, the apostles did more than witness Jesus' life and victory over death. They explained to prospective converts what it *meant* to be a follower of Christ. Christian theology predated the Gospels—and for good reason. Throughout the centuries, Christians would be tempted to embrace the Gospels selectively rather than inclusively—to choose those passages that are most appealing or that support their prejudices, and to downplay or disregard the rest. There would always be a tendency to reject off-the-rack orthodoxy in favor of a "designer" Christianity bearing the individual believer's private label.

Because St. Paul began so early to explain in detail the implications of Christian faith and life, critics have accused him of inventing Christianity—of saddling the simple teachings and example of Jesus with demanding interpretations and directions. To the credit of Paul and the other apostles, any fair-minded reader must acknowledge that the implications of Jesus' teachings are neither simple nor easy nor even crystal clear. Reading a book doesn't make you a Christian, even when that book is the Bible.

It was the Church's responsibility to ensure that Christianity did not degenerate into inspirational philosophy or arcane mysticism. The apostles and their successors were vigilant lest anyone attempt to pass off a fictitious faith as the real thing. From the outset, the Church defended orthodoxy against phony faith. *Heresy* is adherence to beliefs that contradict revelation.

Of course, the Church no longer exiles or executes heretics, but perhaps you can grasp why Christianity took such drastic measures to keep the faith pure: the Church assumed that our salvation was vulnerable to false faith. Today, when secular society has raised tolerance to a virtue in practically every area of life, it is tempting to assume that all we need is a clear conscience to inherit eternal life. The Church answered that the highway to hell is paved with good intentions. To prevent just such slippage, the Church dedicated itself to *educating* the consciences of Christians and, as history illustrates, it proved to be a stern schoolmaster.

When Joan of Arc was brought to trial for the heresy of preferring her private revelations to those sanctioned by the Church, it took two learned judges, fifty experts in law and evidence, and many weeks to give the appearance of a fair trial. Despite all these precautions, the church court found Joan guilty and, when she refused to recant, burned her at the stake. The Church later admitted that the court was politically motivated—and it proclaimed her a saint. Clearly, that decision came too late to benefit Joan, but it dramatically demonstrated the Church's conviction that the substance of faith is critical—that *what* one believes matters.

Heresy and Orthodoxy

My dog-eared copy of G. K. Chesterton's *Orthodoxy* is subtitled "The Romance of Faith." As you know, many human romances are rocky, and some flirt with infidelity. Religious faith is equally vulnerable to temptation. It is no wonder that the Church often finds itself in a position similar to that of the Supreme Court justice who couldn't exactly define pornography but knew it when he saw it. The Church cannot dispel the mysteries underlying faith, but it certainly senses false faith. It was not until the fourth century that the Church proclaimed a Christian creed. That expression of our common beliefs was challenged before and since by revisionists who had different ideas. Many of the tinkerers, if not most of them, were utterly sincere, but they were heretics nonetheless.

Physicians treat diseases and psychiatrists grapple with madness and delusion; their aim is to restore health, which, frankly, isn't nearly as interesting as the myriad maladies they deal with. Similarly, orthodoxy—compared to heresy—is as dull as dishwater. Heresies aim to answer mysteries and clarify Christianity, whereas orthodoxy is typically content with just being precise about what remains mysterious. Because Christianity is so complex—for example, no other religion insists that God is one, yet three—it attracts some people who would cut corners by simplifying the faith. Orthodoxy, for example, insists that Jesus is fully God and fully man, without resolving the puzzle; heresy solves it by proclaiming "take your pick."

Many heresies emerged during times when the Church was complacent or corrupt, advertising themselves as Christian reforms. Reformers typically depict themselves as purer than the institutions they aim to renew. Admittedly, plenty of heretics banished or burned at the stake were morally superior to their executioners (your mother's direct ancestor, the Scottish Catholic bishop who was John Knox's mentor, is an example), but many were also obstinate and intolerant. They were certain that, within Christianity's complexity, there was a simple faith fighting to break out. In one respect, at least, heretical movements had a beneficial effect on Christianity: they forced the Church to be clearer in its teaching, and kept it alert.

One way for you to become clearer and more confident in your faith is to see where former Christians got it wrong. The first "heresy," oddly enough, was proposed by the least likely candidates—the original apostles—who at first treated the Christian faith as a mere refinement of Judaism. Saint Paul, of course, persuaded them of their error and wrested from them an acknowledgment that one could be a Christian without embracing Judaism as well (see Acts 15:10–11). Peter, initially disagreeing with Paul, reluctantly acknowledged that he had converted the Roman centurion Cornelius and his family, and that they were fully Christian without being Jews. Now siding with Paul against the others, Peter argued:

> *Why then must you strain the patience of God by trying to put on the shoulders of these disciples a burden which neither our fathers nor we were able to bear? Surely the fact is that it is by the grace of the Lord Jesus that we are saved by faith, just as they are!* (Acts 15:10–11)

The apostles unanimously agreed to these terms. But to ensure that Gentile and Jewish Christians would not establish competing churches in the cities of the empire, they asked that Gentiles respect Jewish dietary scruples when they dined together—for example, avoiding the meat of strangled animals or those offered to idols.

Early Heresies

The agreement of the apostles to unshackle Christianity from Judaism made it possible to carry out Jesus' command to teach and baptize all nations, creating a universal Church. But there was already a powerful movement that preferred the new faith to be less open and accessible. *Gnosticism* (*gnosis*—"to know"; secret knowledge) doted on mystery and proclaimed the material world to be evil. Christ, the Gnostics claimed, redeemed only those elect who can respond to the divine spark in their minds and escape the earthly prison of their bodies into pure spirit. In his first letter to the church at Corinth, Paul reprimands a Gnostic faction in that community.

Compared to orthodoxy, this early heresy had snob appeal: it was pseudo-philosophical and exclusive, preferring the Church to be a kind of fraternal lodge with restricted membership, arcane rites, and hidden wisdom. Indeed, Gnosticism appealed to supposed sayings of Jesus that, inexplicably, had never been committed to writing.

Perhaps the most pernicious of Gnosticism's tenets was that the physical world was not God's creation, but stood as an impediment to humankind's redemption. Orthodoxy countered that Jesus was the Word made flesh, and that his Resurrection was not just spiritual but physical as well. In the fourth century, when Marcion, a prominent Gnostic, objected to the continued use of the Old Testament by Christians, the Church was forced to uphold the inspiration of the Jewish Scriptures and determine which of the multitude of writings purporting to be Christian revelation deserved to be included in the New Testament. Effectively, the Church created and sanctioned the Bible.

Starting in A.D. 156, *Montanism* attempted to revive the charismatic practices of the Church during the previous century. By the second century, the Church no longer expected the imminent return of Christ and consummation of the kingdom; moreover the apostolic gifts of healing, prophesy, and strange tongues had disappeared. Montanism was not only revivalist in spirit, but intensely puritanical. It demanded celibacy and rigorous fasting of all Christians, and it actively sought martyrdom. Once Christians were baptized, Montanism alleged, there was no further forgiveness for their sins except in the blood of martyrs.

The Church denounced Montanism less for its teachings than for its arrogant elitism. Oddly enough, the most celebrated Montanist, Tertullian, while fanatical in the practice of his personal faith, was orthodox in his teaching and first articulated the doctrine that the Holy Spirit is equally God with the Father and the Son.

Heretical Notions about Jesus

Monarchianism was the first prominent heresy to grapple with the mystery of how Jesus could be both God and man, deciding that the simplest explanation is that he was only an exalted human messiah. This prompted Irenaeus, bishop of Lyon, to insist on the orthodox position that Jesus was fully human and fully divine—that, in Jesus, *God himself suffered* for mankind, demonstrating the extent of his love for his creation.

Arianism proved to be a more subtle and vastly more popular heresy. For a time in the fourth century, its adherents across the empire outnumbered orthodox Christians because of the Arians' simple solution to Jesus' dual identity. Arians acknowledged that Jesus was the Son of God, but only a human creature capable of sin. In short, the Savior was divine not by dint of his own nature but because God willed him to be.

It is probable that Roman Emperor Constantine, a convert to Christianity, had Arian leanings, but likelier still that he considered the controversy to be of only technical importance. In an effort to ensure that the Church was undivided as a bulwark of the newly christianized empire, he assembled two hundred bishops, accompanied by hundreds of other clergy and laity, at Nicaea in A.D. 325 to settle the matter once and for all.

You've heard the popular allegation that history is written by the victors. But in its long conflict with Arianism, orthodoxy was constantly under siege. At Nicaea, the Church forged the statement of Christian beliefs we know today as the Athanasian or Nicene Creed, which proclaimed that Jesus was "true God from true God, begotten, not made, of one substance with the Father." That's the creed we profess each Sunday in church.

Not only the Arians but many of the orthodox were unhappy with the lawyerly language of the creed, especially since the expression "of one substance" appears nowhere in Scripture. Arianism persisted until the eighth century, but it probably lingers in the faith of uncritical Christians who cannot conceive of God the Father and God the Son without the priority of the former and dependence of the latter—just as in human parentage and progeny.

In its successful articulation of a creed meant to counter Arianism, the Church opened the door to the Protestant revolt of the sixteenth century, because those later reformers would insist that the Church had no authority to enunciate doctrines that were not substantiated, chapter and verse, in the Bible.

Attempts abounded to simplify the understanding of how Christ could be both God and man. *Apollinarianism* believed it had the answer when it taught that Jesus had a human body but a divine soul. *Too* simple, the Church replied. This heresy mutilated Jesus' humanity and divinity alike, leaving the Christ only half man and half God.

Nestorianism attempted a further refinement, arguing that, while the human Jesus had a human mother, the divine Jesus had God for his father. Far from solving the mystery of the Incarnation, this new heresy left Jesus with a split personality. Nevertheless, Nestorianism was a lively heresy with a missionary zeal that successfully extended Christianity into the East just as orthodoxy consolidated its hold on Europe. To this day, there are remnants of Nestorians in Iran, Iraq, and the United States.

Viral Mutations

While it is in the nature of orthodoxy to oppose heresy as a disease, the viral infection produces its own unorthodox mutations. In the fifth century, for example, *Monophysitism* aimed to "correct" Nestorianism by claiming that Jesus' divine and human natures were *blended* at the Incarnation, so that henceforth Christ possessed but a single nature, which was divine. The Church answered by saying that to deny Jesus' humanity was to render his suffering a sham and to devalue his life on earth. The new heresy, in short, converted Jesus into God walking about in the guise of a man.

At a distance of two millennia, these controversies seem at best quaint and, at worst, mischievous. But in the age of faith, Christians were steeped in religion. No one took God or Christ for granted because they occupied their every waking moment. To be useful to humankind, God must be interested in humanity's fate. Jesus can be neither God pretending to be a man, nor a man pretending to be God. The Savior's human temptation, suffering, and obedience unto death had to be as real as his eternal reign as Lord. In short, the truth *mattered*.

Nevertheless, there arose an incentive to ending these intramural disputes. A united Islam challenged disputatious Christianity and would threaten the Church for a millennium. To ensure a united Church, Emperor Justinian in the sixth century waged such total war on heresy that thousands of Montanists (in scenes reminiscent of the Branch Davidians in Waco, Texas) sought sanctuary in their churches, set them ablaze, and perished in the flames.

Ironically, Justinian's wife flirted with Monophysitism and contrived to arrest Pope Silverius in A.D. 540 on a charge of treason, replacing him with a more compliant pontiff. But none of these machinations produced an end to heresy. Finally, in A.D. 680–681, tiring of controversy and reeling from the loss of the Middle East and North Africa to Islam, the Church—at the Council of Constantinople—united against the heretics, proclaiming that Jesus had both a divine will and a human will, although always in agreement. To this day, Catholics, Orthodox, and most Protestants agree with the Church's resolution of these disputes. However, Monophysitism persists to the present in the Ethiopian Church.

The State of Orthodoxy

By the late seventh century, the Church had long since promulgated the Apostles' and Nicene Creeds as shorthand summaries of the Christian faith. It had established the equality of the Persons of the Trinity and affirmed Jesus' full divinity and humanity. Moreover, it had settled on which books were to be included in the New Testament and which were to be rejected.

To consolidate these gains, and to provide a bulwark against future heresies, the Church agreed that authority passed in an unbroken line from the apostles, and that the bishop of Rome (or pope), spiritual ruler of the Holy Roman Empire, was the ultimate arbiter of orthodoxy. Papal infallibility about matters of Christian faith and life was not to be employed whimsically or arbitrarily, but only with the assent and support of the whole Church.

These last two safeguards of orthodoxy would be challenged, of course, by the Protestant reformers nearly a millennium later but, taken together with the others, they gave stability to the Christian faith and structure to the Church. The Church was pronounced one, holy, universal, and apostolic. It was holy by dint of being the body and spouse of Christ and the temple of God's Spirit. As an institution, of course, it was subject to the foibles of those who sought salaried careers in its service. Predictably, as the Church became wealthier and more powerful, it occasionally attracted the wrong careerists for the wrong reasons.

It is not surprising, therefore, that later heresies concerned themselves not with God's identity or with Christ's personality, but with human nature. *Pelagianism*, for example, emerged as a movement in the fifth century, asserting that human beings were born innocent and were graced with the natural ability to control their spiritual destiny, even to be utterly sinless. A person's free will, according to this new heresy, was unconditional.

Orthodoxy's most celebrated defender of the age, St. Augustine, wrote thirty-five books combating Pelagianism. He acknowledged that our first parents were created innocent but, having used their freedom to disobey God, committed the original sin, which has flawed human nature ever since. Humanity's goodness, Augustine argued, is achievable only through God's grace.

On the surface, Pelagianism appears to show only the sunny side of human nature, but its darker implications soon became clear. By this heresy's light, Christian baptism was unnecessary since there was no fault for God to forgive. Pelagianism further claimed that Christ's death and resurrection were also unnecessary since humankind required no redemption. Grace was helpful but not required. By Pelagius's reasoning, Adam was only a bad role model—and Jesus was only a good one.

Orthodoxy Hardens

In combating heresy, unfortunately, there is often a tendency for orthodoxy to harden or overstate its position, distorting the truth it holds precious. In the Church's case stated against Pelagianism, for example, it was clear that human beings cannot save themselves. But neither are they depraved (as a few orthodox zealots were inclined to argue), nor does God predestine some sinners to reject his grace, abandoning them to damnation. Oddly enough, Pelagianism survives in puritanism, which believes that worldly success is the reward for righteousness and human tragedy is the punishment for bad choices.

At one significant juncture, the Church agreed to disagree with itself and split into two organizations, both of them orthodox! The pretext for the separation could not have been more arcane. The Western Church chose to incorporate a new phrase into the creed, stating that the Holy Spirit *proceeded* from the Father and the Son. The Eastern Church believed the expression insulted the Spirit, consigning him to a third-rate status in the Godhead. Rather, it preferred that the Spirit be considered to proceed from the Father *through* the Son. On this technicality, the Roman Catholic and the Orthodox Churches have been institutionally separated since A.D. 1054.

Between the beginning of the second millennium and the Protestant Reformation, the Church was beset by moralistic movements which, in their excesses of righteousness, became heretical. The *Waldensians,* for example, aped the apostles by preaching the gospel two by two from door to door, subsisting on charity alone and living exemplary lives. But it was not long before their zeal prompted them to attack the clergy and devalue penance, the Mass, the sacraments, the saints, and even church music as superfluous to Christian life. The pope, while approving of Waldensian spirituality, condemned their disdain for orthodoxy. Yet, the movement maintained vitality for centuries. During the Reformation, surviving Waldensian communities allied themselves with the Calvinist or Reformed Church.

Even more virulent were the *Albigensians.* Like the Waldensians, they were pious in life but heretical in belief, holding the material world to be unredeemably evil and the human body to be the creation of an evil divinity. This led them to conclude that it was evil to give birth to children. By their reasoning, Christ's incarnation, life, death, and resurrection were only illusions, since a good God would never consider taking on sinful human flesh. Life's purpose, according to the Albigensians, was to liberate one's soul from the prison of the body by denying the flesh.

The movement became so powerful in the twelfth century that the Church actually mounted a crusade against it, but offered forgiveness for those who recanted. Lamentably, it was just such pious provocations that gave life to the dreaded Inquisition, which too often persecuted political and personal enemies under the guise of protecting religious orthodoxy. If you recall the well-meaning hearings of the House Un-American Activities after World War II, you'll have the picture. Communism was the "heresy" in those days. But innocent people were hurt in the quest for the guilty.

I suspect that you believe it is more important how people act than what they believe. But unless your beliefs conform to reality, you will have no standards against which to measure your behavior. "Political correctness," for example, is not a moral standard, but just a tactic that consists of not bothering other people. Whereas real morality demands that you respect yourselves and help others.

As it turned out, the Church proved capable of reforming itself without being goaded by heretics. At the same time the Albigensians were threatening Christianity, St. Francis of Assisi and St. Dominic founded perfectly orthodox movements, based on spiritual simplicity and service, that endure to this day.

In hindsight, it is lamentable that the followers of these two saintly friars served the cause of the Inquisition, but it was because they believed that good intentions alone were inadequate and that the truth mattered in Christian faith and life. Unfortunately, the Inquisition was often too quick to spot infections and too harsh in its remedies.

The Reformation

After A.D. 1517, when Martin Luther publicly challenged the Church's abuse of indulgences and caused a floodtide of dissent, it is no longer a simple matter to separate heresy and orthodoxy. It is far easier simply to trace parallel developments within the Roman Catholic Church on the one hand and the Protestant and national churches on the other. The churches not only accused one another of heresy, but new Protestant denominations separated from their parent churches as they developed their own orthodoxies and spiritual cultures. These separations persist at the same time that a worldwide ecumenical movement is bringing the churches together.

I believe that each of you will find confidence no matter where and with whom you worship. Long before the Reformation, the creed and the gospel became the common possessions of all Christians, and the Church was dedicated to worship, prayer, and mutual service. Today, the beliefs shared among Christians are vastly greater than the distinctions between the churches, which are largely cultural and seldom overtly doctrinal. Catholics cannot conceive of Christianity without the sacraments, just as Evangelicals cannot abide Christianity with them. Some denominations worship quietly, others loudly; some ornately, others simply. Pentecostals and Evangelicals sustain a fever pitch of enthusiasm, while Catholics and mainstream Protestants restrain their emotions the better to survive the roller coaster of life's blessings and hardships. Hymns sung in the churches often reflect these preferences, but they are mostly cultural.

There remains, as Chesterton assures us, an orthodoxy underlying these differences. C. S. Lewis called it "mere" Christianity—the rich faith we Christians hold in common. Confident Christians of whatever denomination devote their lives to conforming to the mind and will of their common Redeemer.

In this regard Jesus consoles us all. He was clearly not speaking of any particular denomination when he promised that wherever two or three of us join together in his name, he is there with us (see Matthew 18:20). So don't try to practice your faith alone. Join Christ's family—the Church.

Faithfully,

Your father

Part II

Hope

Base your happiness
on your hope in Christ.

—Romans 12:2

CHAPTER 4

Discover Enchantment

The obedience of Nature is not to be separated . . .
from spirit's own obedience to the Father of Spirits . . .
The evil dream of Magic
arises from the finite spirit's longing
to get that power without paying that price.

—C. S. Lewis

Dear Christina, Lisa, and Virginia,

Have you ever gazed upon a star or dropped a penny in a pond, and then closed your eyes and hoped for the dearest thing in your heart to happen?

As youngsters, you read stories of enchantment, wishing to believe them. You wanted Snow White's prince to save her with a kiss. You wished Beauty to tame the Beast through love and return him to human form. It is not childish to hope. None of us grows so adult that we cease to wish that we will live happily ever after.

As Christians, you live enchanted lives in an enchanted world not of your own making (but a gift from your Creator) and with the certain hope that you will truly live happily ever after. The star of Bethlehem is the one to wish upon, confident that your wish will come true.

Jesus didn't invent enchantment; rather, it came with the Creation. People have been making wishes and hoping against hope since Adam and Eve, and trying to make their dreams come true. Before Jesus worked miracles, there was *magic*.

Actually, there is still a lot of magic in the world—more than ever, in fact—but it goes by other names, such as "technology" or "applied science." Whatever name it answers to, magic's object remains the same: to bend nature to human purposes.

When I plugged in my electric shaver and percolator this morning, then illuminated the house with the flick of a switch, that was magic! When you and I, born wingless and earthbound, cross an ocean through the air, we do it by magic!

The only difference between ancient and modern wizardry is that you and I do not pretend to be magicians ourselves. Someone else supplies modern wonders to us for a price. They are merely more reliable than the wizardry of the past. Then, conjurers were the experts, and audiences were astounded; today we are merely blasé consumers of enchantment. Which, frankly, is a shame.

Confident Christians do not confuse magic and science. Science tells us what we know about the universe and its forces; magic is what we attempt to do with those forces to cover our vulnerability and find comfort, strength, and reassurance. Magic gave people a modest confidence before Jesus gave us certain hope.

Think about the common plight of humankind. We are born more helpless and needy than most creatures, vulnerable to the heat and cold for want of fur, hide, or scales. We come into the world utterly dependent on parents who give us birth, unequipped for physical survival by the instinctive gifts common to lower animals. We are not armed with claws or teeth against predators, but possess only our slowly developing wits. We humans are pretty fragile creatures.

Consider further that, while we are more intelligent than creatures of instinct, we are also more fearful because we are aware of our vulnerability. The human animal both anticipates and remembers pain and feels its agonies more acutely than the beast. Yet, despite these considerable handicaps, we are not only more hopeful than our fellow creatures, but vastly more demanding. Our nearly limitless expectation of fulfillment is our vanity. (Incidentally, if there were no God, those aspirations would be our curse.)

The Need for Hope

A beast has no need of enchantment because it does not hope; it lives in the present. You and I, however, being creatures of anxiety, remembrance, and hope, live simultaneously in the past, present, and future. The Beast in *Beauty and the Beast* was a notable exception. He was enchantment's victim and needed hope (and love) to return to human form. There has never been a time when men and women did not attempt to conjure prospects more favorable to themselves. Stripped of enchantment, life before Christ would have seemed ultimately hopeless—filled with pain, disappointment, and the prospect of oblivion. With Christianity came certain hope.

Whether they are aware of it or not, all confident Christians believe in enchantment—and much more. For the Century of Progress Exposition in Chicago in 1933, G. K. Chesterton provided this inscription for the General Motors Building:

> *The world will never starve for wonders;*
> *but only for want of wonder.*

Chesterton was not speaking of motorcars but of the attitude that regards the universe as an enchanted place and is open to unexpected gifts. A faithful Christian himself, he considered it to be common courtesy to thank the Creator for everyday wonders. Enchantment is the beginning of hope; redemption and the vision of God are our ultimate aspirations.

I am sure that you have encountered people who pretend to affirm only what science teaches, consigning everything else to superstition. Well, they are wrong. Compared to the believer, the science-obsessed lay person is relatively ignorant. What science knows, it maintains as hypotheses constantly subject to revision as new information comes to light.

Granted, no one has succeeded in reviving the flat-earth theory; nevertheless, even a cursory glance at the newspapers reveals that what was scientific "fact" just yesterday is something to be revised or discounted today. The scientific world is an arena of conflicting theories and is content with provisional truths. It is best at describing how things happen; it is hopeless at explaining *why* they happen or, for that matter, how anything came to be in the first place.

Science is premised on an orderly universe. The scientist cannot cope with chaos, nor could you cope if you lived strictly on the basis of what you could prove without a shadow of a doubt. Without faith, there is no hope. All of us, believers and skeptics, survive by force of little faiths that resist corroboration in a laboratory: that our families love us, that we can go through the day without accident, that our health will hold, that the airline will not lose our bags. There are foolish faiths and cockeyed optimists, of course, but no one can survive a day without faith.

Christians maintain that God provided not only the order of the universe, but its purpose as well—its fundamental predictability as well as its unpredictable wonders. Prior to science, and before Christianity, people thought differently. They were inclined to believe that the universe was more whimsical than orderly, as likely to take life as to give it, and to curse rather than bless. It was with such a sense of vulnerability that humans first tried to seek control of their destiny through enchantment.

Do You Believe in Fairies?

Practically every child who has witnessed a performance of *Peter Pan* leaves believing in the existence of small spirits invisible to mere adults. I suspect you were such believers. But even when adult hopes wane in the trials of everyday living, we are inclined to seek enchantment in a world beyond our senses. Sir Arthur Conan Doyle, creator of Sherlock Holmes, having lost a son in World War I and desperate for hope, persuaded himself of the existence of fairies, claiming photographic evidence of their reality. If fairies exist, he reckoned, then so does an invisible spirit world whose powers might restore hope for mortal men and women. Conan Doyle's contemporary, Harry Houdini, was unsuccessful in his attempts to persuade his friend that magic is only illusion, deceiving the senses, and that hope would have to be found elsewhere.

Long before the dawn of Christianity, there was a pervasive belief in a spirit world that possessed power to do humankind good or ill. It was that faith—and consequent hope—that initially prompted the practice of magic. Rest assured, this was not a groundless faith because, setting aside superstition, even today a purely physical explanation of reality does not hold up.

First of all, our senses themselves are notoriously unreliable reporters of reality. Every capable courtroom lawyer knows that whatever a witness has actually observed has undergone internal interpretation. The reality may be something else altogether. As a college student majoring in experimental psychology, I worked with an array of equipment created at Princeton University that produced absolutely credible optical illusions. In classroom experiments, my subjects' senses consistently deceived them, and so did mine.

Over the past four centuries, philosophers have debated whether we grasp physical reality at all with our senses. In the eighteenth century, Bishop George Berkeley argued against his friend Samuel Johnson that all anyone knows is one's *ideas*. The churchman was persuaded that each of us is, in effect, a prisoner of his or her mind. (In reply, the no-nonsense Dr. Johnson kicked a large stone across a London street, persuaded that his kick proved the stone's existence to them both.)

But the bishop had a point. All we know is what we think, and ideas are not the subjects of our senses. We need brains to process our thinking, of course, and ideas may be delivered by minute electrical charges; nevertheless, our thoughts are not themselves physical. Nor are our emotions. You may break out in a sweat from fear, but your perspiration is only a physical reaction to your emotional state, which is not physical at all, but mental.

The Human Spirit

Believers and skeptics alike agree that what distinguishes humans from other creatures is self-consciousness—our thoughts and our emotions. Since none of these traits is physical, what can they be? For want of a better word, we call them *spiritual.*

Even primitive human beings grasped that they were different from the beasts; while they were burdened with thoughts and emotions, the beasts seemed to manage quite well by instinct and senses alone. Predictably, over time, the human spirit sought for kindred spirits within and beyond the world of mere sensation.

From the outset, existence was unpredictable, and human life precarious. Perhaps, primitive humans hoped, the spirits within and behind things might be persuaded to come to their assistance and give them confidence—so they sought enchantment. In ancient times, of course, no one knew why it rained, why crops grew, or why the rivers flowed; but it seemed that there must be some power that bade them to act as they did. Just as humans are moved by will rather than instinct, presumably there was some intelligence that willed the movement of the stars.

Thus magic was born in the attempt to seduce the spirits in the stones, the water, the sky, and the fire to do the bidding of human beings. Over time, magic developed into ritual and pagan religion, eventually featuring a pantheon of spirits allegedly capable of influencing every aspect of human life.

Born into this world of enchantment, Judaism and Christianity accepted the ancient premise that human beings are both physical and spiritual, that their lives are precarious, and that they need hope. What the new faiths *rejected* was that there are fickle spirits to be seduced, insisting instead that there is but one all-powerful creator Spirit from whom all (and only) good comes.

Judaism offered sacrifices to curry God's favor. In its turn, Christianity preferred prayer to sacrifice. What distinguishes religion from magic is that the former is obedient to God. Unlike magic, religion does not seek hope by manipulating nature; rather, it recognizes that one God is lord of the universe and alone has the power and inclination to fulfill human hope.

Does magic work? People clearly have never abandoned enchantment, because our common plight has never been completely resolved despite the wonders of applied science. Technology, after all, is magic brought up to date; the laboratory has only improved on the spells and incantations of the ancients.

To ask whether magic "works" is akin to demanding whether prayers are answered. Nine out of ten of your fellow Americans pray—three-fourths of us pray every day of our lives. We persist in prayer because we need to keep hope alive. We no longer need magic, because we have identified the source of our hope and know that we can count on God, the source of enchantment.

Superstition

Still, some Christians hedge their bets by clinging to superstition, which is the dark side of enchantment. Whereas magic is wily, hopeful, and proactive, superstition is fearful, passive, and ignorant. Unhappily, Christians in earlier centuries were less confident than they were superstitious.

In *A World Lit Only by Fire,* William Manchester paints a depressing picture of credulous Christian life just five centuries ago. At that time, the Mass was celebrated and the Gospels were written in a language few Christians could understand. Medieval Europeans, unlike ancient pagans, felt themselves to be at the mercy of forces beyond their control, victims of black magic. They believed in sorcery, witchcraft, hobgoblins, werewolves, amulets, and spells. Life at the end of the Middle Ages was a perpetual Halloween full of tricks rather than treats.

Many believers during that time acted from fear rather than faith. When a wealthy woman died, for example, her servants emptied every water container in the house to protect her soul from drowning. Before burial, her corpse was protected from any cat or dog that might run across her coffin and transform her remains into a vampire. (How long do you think our black cats, Fred and Ginger, would have survived in those times?) Monastic manuscripts of the time repeatedly reported the birth of the Antichrist, heralding an imminent Day of Judgment. Over time, however, peasants ignored the alarms and spent the Sabbath, after Mass, in recreation. Life was difficult enough for them without anticipating Armageddon.

Still, a permanent cloud of concern hung over daily living, which was considered to be fraught with danger. If the left eye of a corpse could not be made to close, it was assumed to signal the deceased's present torment in purgatory. There were endless taboos: to don a clean white shirt on Friday, to witness a shooting star in the heavens, or to see a will-o'-the-wisp in the swamps or a vulture overhead: all were believed to invite an early death. So, too, a woman foolish enough to do her laundry during Holy Week was neither long for this world nor a promising candidate for the next.

Should thirteen persons dine at the same table, one of them—like Judas at the Last Supper—was expected to disappear from life before the next meal. Likewise, anyone unlucky enough to hear a wolf howl through the night would not see the dawn. Comets and eclipses—wonders to us—were portents of doom to superstitious Christians (which is to say most of them). Of the spirits thought to lurk in the air, a few were benign but the vast majority were considered malevolent and difficult to dispatch—among them, the souls of unbaptized infants, ghouls who fed on cadavers, nymphs who lured knights to death by drowning, dracs that preyed on little children, and wolfmen and vampires who victimized those who strayed from home during the night.

Of course, we hopeful Christians believe in the providence of a benevolent God. But just five centuries ago many Christians thought God to be ineffective against or inattentive to a bewildering array of sinister spirits that contrived to make daily living more anxiety-ridden. Not only did angels and devils lurk in the air, but spirits were thought to reside in every object in nature. Physicians consulted astrologers before surgery or bloodletting, and epidemics and plagues were traced to unfortunate configurations in the heavens.

In a world of Christian superstition, Satan seemed more real and his power more pervasive than that of the Redeemer. Satyrs, incubi, sirens, cyclops, tritons, and giants were believed to be more numerous than the heavenly host and more eager to wield their powers. Unfortunately, instead of correcting superstition, the Church exploited fear of the devil as a more potent motive than the love of God to keep Christians in tow. Faith, in short, was lopsided, and Christian hope teetered on the brink of despair. And when great churchmen (among them Erasmus and Thomas More) worried about witchcraft, it did nothing to reassure less-sophisticated Christians in their hope, but only strengthened superstition.

Magic and Religion

You will frequently encounter people who dismiss your religious faith as a relic of superstition and the persistence of magic. They are mistaken. The association of magic with religion is not only unfortunate but also false. To link sorcery with superstition unfairly discredits the traditional exploitation of nature for human purposes, which was the preoccupation of ancient magic and persists in innovative technology today. Technology is simply magic that works with some consistency. The computer on which I'm writing these lines is surely magical—when it doesn't crash—but its magic has nothing to do with religion.

The great sociologist Sir James Frazier (1854–1941) argued that magic antedated religion and consisted of initiatives to influence the impersonal natural world. Instead, religion, when it emerged, acknowledged that there were supernatural powers behind nature that had personalities.

You needn't believe in the existence of anything beyond nature to seek hope through magic or applied science. But religion rests on faith in the existence of supernatural powers. Magicians work by their own wits, but believers pray for miracles and have hope in providence. Despite this distinction, faith and magic have long since become intertwined in popular estimation. Today, much that was once considered magical is commonplace and "natural." Magic remains *super*natural only until it is explained.

Granted, some persistent happenings still defy explanation, yet it would be rash to label them as either magical or miraculous. Ghosts, for example, have been experienced by so many sophisticated moderns that there is likely some "reality" to them. What is missing is an explanation. Strictly speaking, there is nothing occult about the computer I am using to write these words, despite its extraordinary abilities. I cannot fathom its mysteries, but its human creators can, so I don't bother.

Much practical magic remains to be explained by science without reference to the supernatural. Through the ages, for example, dowsers have used divining rods to discover the presence of water and minerals beneath the earth. Perfectly rational families, on planning a home in the country, will hire a dowser to work his magic before drilling their well—and they are seldom dissatisfied with the results, despite the fact that they (and the dowser) cannot explain the process. They are just content to have a source of water.

Similarly, our local police departments hire psychics and clairvoyants to assist in their murder investigations because these gifted persons are often effective, whatever the explanation. Long ago, as an undergraduate, I successfully duplicated some of the classic Duke University experiments in parapsychology that still defy explanation, making predictions that improved on chance. It seems that many people are a little bit clairvoyant!

Michael Crichton, best-selling author and Hollywood director, was trained as physician and claims to have bent spoons simply with the power of his mind. A panel of the National Institutes of Health recently approved the ancient practice of acupuncture to relieve pain, despite the inability of modern science to determine why the procedure works. There's enchantment out there all right!

Science is not always an improvement on magic. In medicine, for example, laboratories typically fix on certain maladies and synthesize medications to cure illnesses or alleviate their worst symptoms. Scientists, unlike magicians, are not satisfied with just being effective; they insist on knowing *why* their formulas work.

Herbalists are equally sophisticated in their prescriptions, but less demanding of explanations for the effectiveness of their remedies. All medicine has the same objective—health. Homeopathy merely takes a different approach. Drawing on centuries of experience, it identifies the curative powers contained in thousands of plants and minerals. In the past, when a new plant was discovered in explorations around the world, herbalists pondered what it might cure and experimented until they discovered a medical condition for which it was effective.

Homeopathy is more hit-and-miss than modern pharmaceutical science but, in the end, it is just as successful. Preparing potions may remind the three of you of Camelot's Merlin, but now that you know which formulas work, there is no need for hocus pocus. Enchantment is effective.

Hopeful Stirrings

It was not always so, however. The earliest attempts at magic were clumsy and naive. It is likely that the renowned cave paintings at Lascaux in France and Altamira in Spain were attempts by primitive artists to make their hunts more successful. Today, when you draw animals in your art, Lisa, you intend only to capture their appearance and character. But primitive artists believed that their drawings might facilitate the capture of the real beasts! They employed art as magic.

By the Neolithic Age (3,500 B.C.), it was already commonly held that unseen forces influenced every aspect of people's lives. Magicians sought to manipulate these spirits, and priests attempted to propitiate them for humankind's benefit. The natural world, like Aladdin's lamp, was assumed to harbor genies that might be persuaded to do the bidding of human beings, or at least be deterred from doing them harm. Today, we believe that humans have souls as well as bodies; but ancient peoples believed that animals, plants, and minerals also possessed spirits that could be appealed to. The trick was to gain access to the world of the spirit, and it was often attempted by means of trance-like states and repetitive rites.

The sheer numbers of ancient phallic stones around the world bear witness to prehistoric man's hope to perpetuate life. For the ancient Hindus, the sexual act itself was considered sacramental—just as marriage is today by many Christians. In ancient times, much magic was focused on ensuring fertility, in families as well as fields.

In gathering material for a recent book, psychiatrist Dr. M. Scott Peck devoted months to exploring prehistoric sites in the British Isles. You recognize Stonehenge from photos, but it is only the most-celebrated of the stone structures aimed at enchantment that litter the landscape in Europe, the Mediterranean islands, Africa, Asia, the Middle and Far East, as well as Mexico and Peru. Monoliths in the Andes and gigantic stone heads on Easter Island continue to fascinate—if not educate—us about our ancestors' perennial quest for hope through enchantment.

More recent finds include the foundations of vast circular temples once employed to command the spirits of nature. Their careful construction suggests that they served stable communities, and that magic had already become enmeshed with religion. These structures are clearly too permanent for the use of tent-show magicians; rather, they suggest devotion and propitiation, which are earmarks of religion. The temples were the precursors of our churches.

Faith and the Fates

In ancient Egypt, enchantment and faith were entwined. Pagan priests ruled the nation, employing magic as a ploy to maintain political power. The pharaoh was assumed to influence the elements and the flow of the life-giving River Nile. Embalming and burial rites were contrived to cheat death and to ensure eternity. The Egyptians who wrapped the mummies and constructed the pyramids knew enchantment and possessed hope.

Astrology was probably developed in ancient Babylon, based on a surmise that the planets controlled the destinies of individual men and women. The ancients believed that their fate was writ in the heavens. The Chaldeans were ruled from the city of Ur by magician-kings presumed to have power over the growth of crops. (I once received a writing award that consisted of a statuette of the Egyptian god Thoth, who was also the ancient deity of magic!)

As early as 400 B.C., writings known collectively as the *Hermetica* taught that life consists of a permanent conflict between matter and spirit, and that humans can escape victimhood and obtain hope through hidden knowledge. As I mentioned in my last letter, these notions insinuated themselves into early Christianity by way of the Gnostic heresy, but were eventually purged from the Church.

To this day, however, Masonic, Mormon, and Rosicrucian rites perpetuate the notion of such esoteric wisdom, and the tradition continues (albeit highly diluted) in the rituals of fraternal societies and campus sororities and fraternities. My own college fraternity paid lip service to its nineteenth-century founders' fantasy that the use of skulls, capes, and candles would somehow give the brothers a leg-up on life. It was all pretty silly, but fun.

Simon Magus, a magician mentioned in the New Testament, sought unsuccessfully to purchase the miraculous powers wielded by the apostle Peter. He even aped Jesus' ascension, only to be crippled when he crashed to the ground, the victim of gravity. Undeterred, the magician predicted that he, like Jesus, would die, be buried, and rise again on the third day. In fact, he was never heard from again. Still, it's understandable why the legendary Lawrence of Arabia dismissed Christianity. He associated Jesus with charlatans like Simon, whom he encountered during his exploits in the Middle East. Of course, Jesus was no magician, but his miracles seemed magical.

The persistence of the ancient notion of life as a perpetual war between good and evil had two lamentable consequences. First, the physical world, prone to corruption and decay, was judged to be inferior to the world of the spirit. Second, demonic forces were given equal billing with God and the forces of good. By this measure, life was an endless contest between beneficent and malevolent antagonists, and humanity was the ball they kicked around. Unfortunately, from time to time, popular Christianity has acted as if the material world is the source of sin and Satan the prince of our world.

On the whole, though, Christianity fought to expunge magic from religious hope, while Islam sometimes welcomed it. Even today, when we think of magic, it is often in the imagery of the *Thousand and One Nights*. In the Middle Ages, occultism even became a powerful force in Judaism, although it failed to penetrate orthodox Jewry. The *Kabalah* of the Jews, books prominent in Spain and Provence in the twelfth and thirteenth centuries, incorporated mystical lore—secrets supposedly given to Moses by God which the prophet chose not to reveal to all of the chosen people, but only to select Jews.

The Caballists held that any influence on one part of the world resonates throughout the universe. To achieve their salvation, initiates were required to make an inward journey within a circle drawn to keep out evil spirits. They must pass ten forces controlling the universe, confronting good and evil alike, before reaching the deity who could grant their wish; then they must retrace their perilous journey home. The very complexity of such a trek to redemption ensured that it would never appeal to the mass of Jews or to those of other religious faiths.

The Persistence of Enchantment

Although barbaric Europe was converted to Christianity, it was not wholly weaned from its pagan reliance on enchantment. In fact, barbarians were impressed with what they took to be Jesus' own magic—his ability to walk on water, turn water into wine, multiply fish and bread, cure the sick, raise the dead, and cast out demons. If Jesus' "magic" offered surer hope than their own pagan efforts, they were ripe for conversion!

The Church replied that miracles are the work of God, not magicians. But to the common Christian of the Middle Ages, the distinction was moot. Indeed, the Pharisees had accused Jesus of working magic—"He expels these spirits because he is in league with Beelzebub, the chief of the evil spirits!" (Luke 11:15). It was difficult to persuade rude Christians that saints' relics differed much from ancient amulets, since their use was similar—to ward off misfortune and secure hope.

The Arthurian legends exemplified the coexistence and intermingling of faith and magic in the Dark and Middle Ages. Merlin was not a Christian priest but a magician, and Morgan la Fay was an enchantress with witchlike powers. The Christian King Arthur extracted Excalibur from the stone's grip more by magic than by faith. In Celtic lands to this day a belief in enchantment survives more or less comfortably with Christianity.

In its attempt to supplant paganism and its magical practices, Christianity demolished temples and erected churches on their sites, using the leftover materials for construction. The great cathedral of Chartres in France, for example, was purposely built on the site of a former Druid center. But in the popular mind, the practice of replacing temples with churches only suggested that Christianity wielded a surer magic than paganism.

The great Crusades, aimed at turning faith into chivalry, had the unintended effect of importing classical magic and Arabian occultism into Europe to mix with tribal superstition. As great medieval universities were founded, alchemy and astrology became part of the curriculum. For centuries it remained respectable to attempt to turn base metals into gold, and to discover one's fortune in the movement of the planets.

Saint Thomas Aquinas (1225–1274), the great scholastic philosopher and theologian, reluctantly sanctioned this study, but only to clarify the distinction between miracles and magic. The latter, he argued, was diabolical. Ironically, however, Aquinas believed alchemy to be a respectable science. The condemnation of alchemy by Pope John XXII and Pope Innocent VI merely drove the practice underground in the late Middle Ages, and popes of the period remained ambivalent about astrology.

The popular practice of enchantment was revived during the Black Death of the fourteenth century. Christian priests were hard-pressed to explain how horrendous plagues could be justified as punishments when they killed innocent children as well as sinful adults. In the absence of a persuasive explanation (or healing miracles), anxious Christians reverted to amulets and preventive potions such as powder of dried toad, alcohol, and arsenic—prescriptions worthy of the witches in Shakespeare's *Macbeth.* Some Christians sought hope in pilgrimages to the shrines of saints, seeking their intercession with God.

In succeeding centuries, magic survived in the form of witchcraft, trapping the Church in a dilemma: if Christianity condemned and punished witchcraft, it could hardly declare it to be bogus. In a sense, confident Christians today find themselves in a similar position. Your experience illustrates that evil and good are equally real. But if God is the source of good, then evil must have its own personal source. Deviltry, in short, requires a devil. The Faust legend suggests that Satan stands ready to serve those who cannot bend God to their wishes. Black magic continues to attract the desperate and the rebellious.

Of course, white magic has persisted as well, but the Church resisted making distinctions of color and lumped all enchantment with witchcraft—and much confusion resulted. During the Middle Ages, the saints, once considered to be wholly compassionate, were increasingly thought to be equally inclined to condemn the petitioner! In the Dracula legend, the cross, the sacred host, and holy water prove to be effective in deterring vampires. Predictably, in the late Middle Ages, superstitious Christians employed the cross and holy water as talismans. Instead of consuming the host at Mass, for example, some preserved it as a love charm, hoping to make themselves invisible so they could steal successfully, cure fever, or even inspire bees to make honey.

The Reformation blamed these medieval superstitions on the Catholic Church and stripped Christian worship of priests, saints, indulgences, relics, icons, and holy water, as well as the incomprehensible language of worship—Latin. Still, Protestantism failed to divorce magic altogether from faith. Some Protestant ministers confessed to using charms and spells to cure illnesses and exorcise devils. Moreover, Protestantism retained the Catholic belief in witchcraft.

As you know, your mother dresses as a witch every Halloween to thrill the trick-or-treaters who come to our door. She looks pretty sinister, but maintains to the neighborhood children that she works only white magic. In former centuries, despite her protestations, she would have been suspect and feared by adults as well as children.

Unlike pre-Christian pagan rites, which were communal, witchcraft was a solitary pursuit. Witches' covens were rare, not least because of church opposition and public apprehension. In all likelihood, those accused of witchcraft were probably eccentric, solitary women attempting to cure by natural medicine and charms. Sometimes, they made things worse. As a young girl in Ireland, your great-grandmother Minnie Hayes was blinded for life by such a woman, who attempted to cure her eye infection with poultices.

When Reginald Scot (1538–1599) published a book arguing that witches were only deluded women, King James I had it burned by the public hangman. But by the late seventeenth century, popular belief in witchcraft began to decline, although faith in luck and misfortune appears to be ineradicable. Public sentiment did not turn against the persecution of witches until the eighteenth century. Predictably, the Age of Reason succeeded in expunging many lingering superstitions from religion, but it hardly put a dent in magic. Contemporary New Age thinking is only old magic in new clothing. No longer subject to the constraints of church, and divorced once again from religion, magic today is as close as your telephone's "psychic connections" and the horoscope in your daily newspaper.

I predict that your life of faith will contain magical moments. Enchantment is already abundant in God's creation if you are receptive to it. But there is no need for confident Christians to plot their lives by means of the tarot deck or ouija board. Faith needs no sorcery. Continue, if you wish, to believe in fairies, but count on Christ.

Faithfully,

Your father

CHAPTER 5

Expect Miracles

The central miracle asserted by Christians
is the Incarnation.
They say that God became Man.
Every other miracle prepares for this,
or exhibits this,
or results from this.

—C. S. Lewis

Dear Christina, Lisa, and Virginia,

On May 5 in the year 2000, the sun, the moon, and the five planets visible to the naked eye were in alignment. This entirely natural and predictable event marked Year One of the new millennium. Understandably, many persons assigned extraordinary significance to this heavenly conjunction, as portending either the end of time or the dawning of a new age. The celestial event confirmed the hope of optimists and the despair of pessimists. Yeasayers and naysayers alike heralded the event as miraculous, and they were all wrong.

Miracles are neither natural nor predictable, nor even necessarily spectacular, but they have real significance. Unlike magic, they are not the work of humans, but of God, ensuring that these wonders are not self-serving but benevolent. By definition, miracles are exceptional, the products of our Creator continuing his connection to his creation for its own good. Although you may never witness a miracle, you can believe confidently in them, because they are signs that God not only creates but cares for his creation. Despite their rarity, miracles tell us something good about God. Even more than enchantment, miracles are cause for hope. Miracles are unexpected graces. Grace perfects nature; indeed, it improves *human* nature.

Of course, miracles are also the subject of superstition: fodder for the supermarket tabloids that weekly trumpet tales of weeping statues, heavenly apparitions, ghostly prophesies, and astounding cures. Some Protestant Christians believe that the age of miracles has passed—that they were signs of God's revelation and ceased altogether when that revelation was completed. Many others believe that miracles have never ceased. Indeed, in the Catholic Church, miracles are *required* for a person to be declared a saint.

Miracles and Prayer

Many more people pray than wish upon stars. As I have said, if we can believe them, three out of every four Americans profess that they pray every day of their lives. Although you routinely pray to express your love for God, to thank him, and to ask his forgiveness, on those special occasions when you make a request of God, you are in fact asking for a miracle—only a *tiny* miracle, as a rule, but a miracle nonetheless. The very act of praying presumes that God is ready to intervene in the natural course of events on your behalf. Even when you pray "thy will be done," you are acknowledging that God's will is more important than the normal course of events in your lives, and you are aligning your wills with his.

Despite the fact that the vast majority of Americans pray daily for God's intervention, there are those who dismiss miracles altogether. To give the skeptics the benefit of the doubt, it really is impossible to ascertain, after the fact, that a rare occurrence was miraculous. It is far easier to label the event a quirk of nature, cause unknown but open to explanation according to purely natural causes. A mystifying cure may be no more than that—a mystery. But in the presence of faith and prayer, the same event likely will be deemed miraculous by the person cured and by the person who prayed for the cure. Whether the restoration of health was natural or supernatural, it is only good manners to be grateful to God for his providence.

People who refuse to acknowledge miracles are usually prompted by an aversion to admit any influence over nature besides their own. Atheists insist that nature is self-contained, self-maintained, and self-generated. This, of course, is only an assumption, and unbelievers must content themselves with the incredible notion that nature somehow created itself or always was. This is an odd view of eternity, but it insulates the skeptic from acknowledging any dependency on a Creator.

Miracles threaten the skeptic's conviction that whatever is only *happens* to be, and has no external cause. Whereas confident Christians trace their origin to God, dogmatic atheists credit their existence to the dumb workings of nature. How unthinking and unfeeling nature could produce a rational and passionate person with a hankering for eternity is a question they choose not to answer. Should they be pressed to venture an opinion, it will be that thoughts and emotions are only electrical charges in the human brain. (But if that is true, how can we know that our ideas and loves are true rather than false?)

Although a scientist may believe in miracles, miracles are, nonetheless foreign to science, because they stand outside natural explanation. In point of fact, many scientists resist the supernatural altogether because it is ultimately elusive. To live in a universe that admits of miracles, some scientists concede, would be to wallow in chaos, because science is based on predictability, which assumes that nature operates with regularity. Scientists are wary of exceptions, and miracles are precisely exceptional (but providential as well). It is of the nature of miracles that people welcome them.

An Interfering Father

Miracles even offend some Christians who maintain that, by choosing to interfere with nature, God is admitting that he failed to create it correctly in the first place. Many rationalists are ready to acknowledge a God who set the universe in motion at the outset and then retired to his heaven, but they resist the notion of a Father who maintains concern for his creatures. Often their reluctance merely reflects their discomfort with a personal God butting into their private lives. Make no mistake: miracles can be unsettling because they reveal God to be interested in his creation and active in shaping it. As Francis Thompson writes, the Hound of Heaven does not leave us alone, an intrusive fact that may annoy some but that offers you hope.

Environmentalists worry that, without governmental intervention, nature will fall prey to humanity's predatory instincts and eventually cease to serve it. Doubtless, nature is fragile and vulnerable to change, but no one seriously proposes that it is in danger of ceasing to exist altogether. When Christians contemplate the end of the world, we think of it as a series of dramatic events and transformations, not as dissolution and oblivion. In this respect, we supernaturalists agree with naturalists—that nature, once constituted, cannot be destroyed but only altered for better or worse.

But have you ever considered that it is every bit as likely that nature continues to exist at every moment only because God wills it? By this measure, God did not simply create nature and leave the universe to its own devices; rather, the stars, planets, flora, and fauna must be maintained in existence. That does not demand the

Creator's miraculous intervention, of course, but it does require his constant concern. For all we know, the universe might cease to exist if God stopped thinking about us. In any case, it is precisely because God has not wholly retreated to his heaven that all is well with the world.

Because God lives in eternity, he is not confined to past, present, and future time as you and I are, nor is he burdened by the weight of memory and the anxiety of anticipation. He is eternally young, living in the present, free of the vagaries of time. We call his intrusions into time "miracles." They change the world without changing him—and they change it for the better.

Why Miracles Are Needed

But why should God's tinkering be needed at all? In other words, why didn't a perfect God create a perfect world in the first place? In Voltaire's famous story, *Candide,* his naive hero wanted to believe that ours is the best of all possible worlds. In the end, Candide's misadventures convinced him otherwise. Were you gods, you would surely make improvements to God's creation. Well, miracles are *his* improvements, and the Incarnation—God becoming one of us in Jesus—was the greatest improvement imaginable. We cannot pretend to penetrate divine providence, but we can be sure that we are part of his eternal plan that is unfolding.

As you might suspect, evil is at the root of life's shortcomings, and God is not its author. In addition to God's will, there are billions of human wills at work in the world, and some of them are malevolent. Whereas typical medieval Christians suspected Satan to be the source of their daily misfortunes, you and I are more likely to assign the blame to other people for the misfortunes we suffer.

The century in which you were born testifies to the inhumanity of humans to humans. Despite unprecedented advances in health, comfort, convenience, and longevity, the twentieth century was one of worldwide conflict. For the past one hundred years, human nature was repeatedly tested—and repeatedly failed. Its gulags, ethnic cleansings, and holocausts did not prompt the question, "How can miracles be?" but rather, "Why can't we count on more of them?" When God intervenes, it is because he gave humans the freedom to be perverse, and too many of us have used our liberty to victimize one another.

To be sure, there is another kind of evil people do not perpetrate, but simply suffer. Cancer is perfectly awful, but is also perfectly *natural;* so are diseases, plagues, and famines that happen in the course of nature. Insurance companies unkindly call some catastrophes "acts of God" (to avoid paying the victims); in reality, they are but mere natural occurrences that wreak havoc and cause destruction. Because nature, unlike you and me, is unfeeling and unthinking, we sometimes find ourselves its victims. Nature has no compunction. Fire not only warms, but burns. Water slakes thirst, but can drown. A breeze refreshes, but a tornado devastates.

Could God have made fire that warms without scorching, water that refreshes but does not drown, or wind that blows gently but never destructively? We do not know, and it is an idle question in any case. From the dawn of human history, thinking men and women have striven to become thoughtless nature's masters instead of its victims. It is our job to tame nature. When we fail at mastery we pray for miracles.

Accidents

There is yet another source of evil in the world: sometimes people find themselves in the wrong places at the wrong times and become the victims of events. For example, when lightning strikes randomly, superstitious people call this randomness fate or misfortune, but it is really nothing more than a tragic accident. The recent popularity of "no fault" insurance reflects the common experience that, when bad things happen to good people, sometimes no one is responsible for the damage. The rain falls on the just and the sinner alike (see Matthew 5:45). It can end a drought or spoil a picnic.

Of course, good things can happen by accident as well, and you may be tempted to consider them as *providential*—not miraculous interventions exactly, but part of God's plan. I confess that I myself have felt that way at times. But C. S. Lewis rejected this kind of selective providence, contending that *everything* that happens is providential because God never slackens in his attention. He does not look in on his creation only in time of crisis, but is ever present.

Sophisticated skeptics maintain that prayer is pointless because God has already made up his mind eternally. What these naysayers neglect to note is that God has eternally taken our prayers into consideration as well. So you will not change your Creator's mind with your prayers, but those prayers were factored into God's providence even before time began! He has known all along that you would pray, and he has known from all eternity that he will care for you. In a sense—*God's sense*—our prayers precede us.

Because he is unfettered by time, God did not create the universe "long ago," but creates it at every moment. Prayer is a call upon our Creator and an acknowledgment of our utter dependency on him, but it is not magic. We do not bend God to our wills; rather, we attempt to conform our wills to his. We pray for miracles because we know he wills what is good for us. That is the basis of our hope.

Every Christian, confident or timid, realizes that prayers are not always answered, certainly not with the precise answers we seek. Nevertheless, they are *heard* and are taken into consideration. If prayers were sure things, we would be magicians, and God would be putty in our hands. Rather, prayer is a call upon God's benevolence—our request for a miracle.

Nature *belongs* to God, just as we do. He can do what he wishes with nature and with us. God is Creator of nature and supernature alike; for him, there are no distinctions. An angel—or a devil, for that matter—is as real to God as you and I are to him and to one another. You must grant God his miracles. He is like a weekend mechanic with a classic automobile, forever fussing with it because it is precious to him, even when it already runs pretty well. God intends the world—and us—to run even better than we do.

Miracles in the Bible

Oddly enough, the word "miracle" does not appear in the Bible. Instead we are told of "signs," "wonders," "portents," "works of power," or simply "works." In the Old Testament, the most impressive miracles are those surrounding the deliverance of the Jews from Egypt to the promised land. In the New Testament, there are many more miracles, worked by Jesus as well as his disciples. In every instance, it is God's power, not human power, at work, and no miracle is merely frivolous. Each has a particular purpose. Taken together, they have an overarching purpose: not to put on a show but to make a point. In the Old Testament, that point is to show God's faithfulness; in the New Testament, it is to proclaim the good news of Christ.

Miracles confirm the cliché that actions speak louder than words. Yet, Jesus was clearly a reluctant miracle worker. He was never prodigal with his powers. In fact, he often sought no audience and, on occasion, told those he cured to keep silent about their blessing. Overall, Jesus employed his miracles to validate his mission to forgive sins and usher in the Kingdom of God.

At the outset of his ministry, when followers of John the Baptist asked him who he was, Jesus told them to return to John and tell him what they had seen and heard: "The blind are recovering their sight, cripples are walking again, lepers being healed, the deaf hearing, dead men are being brought to life again, and the good news is being given to those in need" (Luke 7:22).

Miracles illustrate the good news of our salvation—our cause for hope—but they are calls for faith in something beyond the miracles themselves. For example, when Jesus acknowledged the faith of a paralyzed man, he declared, "My son, your sins are forgiven" (Mark 2:5), prompting an outcry from Jesus' critics that only God can forgive sins.

> *Jesus realized instantly what they were thinking, and said to them, "Which do you suppose is easier—to say to a paralyzed man, 'Your sins are forgiven,' or 'Get up, pick up your bed and walk'? But to prove to you that the Son of Man has full authority to forgive sins on earth, I say to you,"—and here he spoke to the paralytic—"'Get up, pick up your bed and go home'"* (Mark 2: 9–11).

The purpose of this miracle was not to demonstrate Jesus' powers as a healer, but to show that faith in Jesus is a call on God's power. If being reconciled to God is more important than the ability to walk and move, then it is precious, indeed, and the very point of Jesus' ministry. As a young child, I wondered why Jesus, with his obvious powers, did not work many more miracles. It was only later that I grasped that God did not become man to fix all the glitches in creation, but rather to reconcile all of creation to himself.

The Purpose of Miracles

Because we pray for miracles, we assume we know what they mean. After all, we wouldn't ask for them if they didn't suit our purposes. But in the Bible, miracles suit

God's purposes and are intended to be learning experiences for us. The question we should ask of every miracle is "What is God's message imparted through this event?" For instance, in the Old Testament God employs miracles to *confirm* his choice of persons such as Abraham, Jacob, and Moses, to *judge* those who resist him, to *show mercy* by meeting human needs, to *deliver* captives, and to *disclose* his intentions. In each case, miracles draw attention to God's perpetual providence. They are cause for confidence and hope.

In the New Testament, miracles draw attention to who Jesus is and what he came to accomplish. Most people regard Jesus as an appealing man and a wise teacher, but some resist his miracles as somehow cheapening his message. What they overlook is that Jesus was not a philosopher, debating wise thoughts and setting a good example, but the Son of God calling for repentance, promising redemption, and inaugurating the Kingdom of God. These ultimate wonders called out for particular miracles to confirm Jesus' mission.

Jesus served not only as the subject but also as the object of his first miracle (his Incarnation) and his last (his Resurrection). Those miracles are like bookends, containing between them a life like no other creature's before or since, demonstrating that he was a man like no other, one who merits our faith not for what he can do for us but for who he is.

In between those ultimate miracles, Jesus worked others, commanding nature and supernature, stilling the waters, and expelling demons. By contrast, the heroes of the Old Testament were only instruments of God's power; their wonders were not nearly as personal as those wrought by Jesus. For example, many Old Testament miracles were produced by instruments—rods, trees, and mantles—whereas Jesus worked his miracles by a word or a touch. Moses had to plead with God to cure his sister's leprosy (see Numbers 12:13), but Jesus cured lepers by touch and even at a distance (see Luke 17:12). Elisha sent a leper to the Jordan to be cleansed (see 2 Kings 5:17), whereas Jesus restored the health of a soldier's servant without even being near him (see Matthew 8:5).

In the Old Testament, the God of the Jews established himself among his people as king over a theocracy. Miraculously, he built his kingdom and destroyed his nation's enemies. Although the God of the Jews was feared and admired because of his works, his favor was attributed to his mercy. Psalm 136 chronicles the miracles of deliverance in the Old Testament. Yahweh is clearly a warrior God, yet each verse of the psalm fittingly concludes with the phrase: "His love endures forever."

Miracles as Acts of Love

The God of the Jews, often characterized as angry and vengeful, was, in fact, praised for his loving interventions. Unlike Jesus' miracles, which typically benefited individuals and smaller groups, the wonders of the Old Testament uplifted an entire nation. The psalmist praises God for being the one God the Jews can depend on. He is called loving because he is Creator, Deliverer, Defender, Leader, Lawgiver, and Conqueror, and because he gave his people their land, their freedom, and their abundance. This is not just idle praise for divine providence, but an acknowledgment that God has acted, time and time again, miraculously and mercifully, for his people.

When Jesus entered history as a member of this chosen people, these former wonders colored their expectations of the Messiah. Revealingly, Jesus did not seek to duplicate them. He did not create, deliver, lead, or conquer. Nor did he attempt to restore the Jews' land, freedom, or abundance. Instead, he forged an entirely new covenant, no longer based on power, property, law, or national origin, but on repentance, faith, and love.

Compared to Moses, who was a mere man but who led an entire nation out of exile, parting the Red Sea to ensure their passage, the divine Jesus was unpretentious. He began his ministry alone in the desert, choosing twelve ordinary men to be his cohort. In the main, he spoke to individuals and to small groups, rarely to multitudes, and never to the nation.

Jesus spoke to the heart—and nations do not possess hearts; only individuals do. Jesus asked for a *change* of heart, a personal turning to God and faith in his power to forgive and save. Jesus' miracles suited his mission. They delivered individuals from their maladies and their personal demons, and from death itself. They demonstrated Jesus' power over nature, always in ways that benefited individuals: feeding the hungry multitudes, calming the waters that threatened to drown his companions, turning water into wine to save his friends from embarrassment at their wedding reception. Jesus' wonders were miracles of courtesy.

There was one rare spectacle, when Jesus was glorified on a mountaintop, his face shining like the sun. But even that splendid show lacked a large audience and was intended only to reassure his few fickle followers. Despite the star of Bethlehem and the three kings, Jesus' birth could not have been less ostentatious. Finally, when he rose from the dead, there was neither spectacle nor self-vindication, no proclaiming "I told you so." At the moment of Jesus' death, it is related that the sky over Jerusalem darkened, the curtain of the Temple was torn from top to bottom, and the bodies of the dead were seen in the streets—illustrating that nature took note of Jesus the miracle worker, while the nation yawned and forgot.

You probably assume that Jesus was able to perform miracles because he was God, but some theologians speculate that his power may have come from being a perfect *human being*. Here's their reasoning: if the original fall from grace means anything, it signifies more than exile from Eden. Original sin affected human nature at its core, leaving each of us with a kind of moral schizophrenia and radical lack of integrity. We're no longer totally "together." We experience our human condition every day, acknowledging the character flaws within ourselves and others. As Christians, we believe that our innocence was lost long before you or I were born.

Recall that in the Genesis account, God gave the first man and woman *dominion* over the creatures and the garden. It's only speculation, but for all we know, their original innocence may have enabled them to exercise that responsibility through miracles! Saints perform miracles because they have returned to the innocence of Adam, and God's power is free to flow through them for the good of the rest of us. So it is at least worth speculating that Jesus, the perfect man and the New Adam, exercised dominion over nature through his human nature. You may consider it far-fetched, but it is not an idle thought. Redeemed and returned to your Creator, you will have your innocence and original powers restored. In eternity, *you* will be miracle workers!

The Meaning of Jesus' Miracles

C. S. Lewis divides the miracles of Jesus into two categories: those that repeat what God had done before, and those of the New Creation. In the former are acts of fertility, healing, dominion over the inorganic world, and miracles of destruction. In the latter, Jesus breaks entirely new ground, restoring life and perfecting and glorifying nature itself.

When Jesus turns water into wine, for example, the only wonder is that the transformation is instantaneous. After all, God creates the ingredients of wine through nature all the time, but normally it takes a season for water to nourish the vines and make the grapes and at least another season to ferment. The end product (wine) is the same, and its agent (God) is the same. The *miracle* consists in speeding up the process of winemaking!

Similarly, when Jesus fed the multitudes with a few loaves and fishes, he was only doing what the Creator has been accomplishing all along—multiplying seeds that turn into wheat and spawns that become schools of fish. The only wonder is that the Son did it in an instant rather than in his Father's good time.

Competent physicians will admit that they do not really heal the human body when it is unhealthy, but only assist nature to restore health. The ultimate wonder does not reside in surgery or prescription drugs, but in the human body, whose tissues repair themselves and fight disease naturally. God created our bodies with built-in healing mechanisms. That means that he has been in the healing business all along. What is miraculous about Jesus' acts of healing is that they were instantaneous and augmented the body's natural healing powers.

When Jesus miraculously caused the withering of the fig tree, his point was metaphorical: to demonstrate God's judgment on people's faith at the time—that it was fruitless. But in actually destroying the tree, he was only doing what God had been doing since the dawn of creation: presiding as lord of life and death. Death provides the soil for new life. Again, what was miraculous about the withering of the fig tree is that Jesus accomplished it promptly at his command. But, as C. S. Lewis affirms, not a single tree died that year in Israel or anywhere else on earth except for God's action or inaction.

To take another example, when Jesus calmed the storm, he merely demonstrated, in an instant, what God always does: manage the elements that create climatic conditions. But here's a departure: when Jesus walked on water, he did something God had never done. Christ did not simply short-circuit nature or demonstrate God's providence. He *changed* the very properties of water so it would support his weight. He miraculously *transformed* nature, giving the first inkling of his ability to form a New Creation to be the consummate source of hope and confidence for you and me. The New Creation will be the subject of my next letter.

The Miracle of Faith

You believe as Christians, because your mother and I raised you in our faith and because the nation you live in was founded on that tradition. Faith responds to our sense of mortality, our hunger for integrity, and our attraction to a God who cares for our welfare. Normally, along with that faith comes hope. For a few persons, however, faith itself requires a miracle.

Consider St. Paul, the recipient of one of the more painful miracles on record. With a bolt of lightning, God blinded Paul and called him to account. As miracles go, Paul's was not comforting, but it was effective. He became the principal missionary to the world beyond Israel.

Unfortunately, miracles, sometimes prove to be stumbling blocks, giving our faith the appearance of fantasy to skeptics. Nor do miracles satisfy superstitious people, who are more interested in tricking fate and finding fortune than in seeking God's will. Miracles do not answer the demands of people who merely wish to be lucky, because God's wonders are rare, unpredictable, and providential. They are God's property, not ours.

By definition, miracles are exceptions, whereas faith is unexceptional. We do not base our faith on an exception, and we do not bargain with God when he holds all the cards. More often than not, the miracles you and I seek won't be delivered in the form we seek them, but you need never feel that you have prayed in vain. Happily, hope grows despite disappointment; that may be what is truly miraculous.

Michael Watkins, an English travel writer, is a self-proclaimed atheist, but when he paid a visit to Lourdes in France, he found himself caught up in the faith of his terminally ill fellow countrymen who were there seeking miracles. Watkins described his experience in the Sunday *Times*:

> *I had never been on a religious pilgrimage before, and didn't know what to expect. I had thought about Lourdes, but in the abstract way that I thought about clearing out my attic: the day would come, but not yet. Both Lourdes and the attic might contain things I shouldn't know what to do with, so they could wait . . .*
>
> *The grotto was packed . . . from early morning until late night. They were the raggle-taggle of Europe and beyond; they were down at the heel and looked worn out, exhausted by factory and field, and by despair. Some were very ill. There were thousands of them and I thought: I've never heard so many people make such a silence. . . .*
>
> *The little girl in our group, the one with leukemia, was called Anne; I was offered the job of pushing her wheelchair . . . If you have ever seen 40,000 or so pilgrims, each holding a candle and singing the Ave Maria, it may be hard to understand Anne's pleasure. Suddenly, she shivered. I put my pullover around her and her mother hugged her. Afterwards Father Dickie and I opened a bottle of whisky in my room. We didn't say much, we drank instead. We needed it. . . .*
>
> *I'd come to Lourdes as a spectator, not a participant; I had no intention of becoming involved. But it did not work out like that. I was pushing a little girl with leukemia to be blessed, and I wasn't bearing up very well. Not much good at praying, I was having a go for Anne; and it made my eyes so hot I could hardly see where I was going.*

Anne was not favored with a miraculous cure, but Watkins now believes in miracles because she did.

Miracles aren't just for us Christians. A few years ago, *Washington Post* columnist Jeanne Marie Laskas interviewed a woman who claimed to have witnessed a statue of the elephant god, Ganesh, drinking milk in her Silver Spring, Maryland, temple—an occurrence reported with some regularity by Hindus elsewhere around the world. The purported miracle prompted Laskas, raised a Christian, to reflect:

> *To her, the miracle was a reminder that her god was alive and well. And, in that way, a reminder that her belief was, too. . . . The longer you live in a world that demands to know how much, how soon, how fast, the harder it is to grasp the infinite. Maybe you believe it and maybe you don't. But maybe it triggers something. A memory of when the leap of faith was not so difficult. And then you know it is possible. You have the ability to leap.*

I wish you happy leaping and confident hoping. Expect miracles!

Faithfully,

Your father

Chapter 6

Be Transformed

The specifically Christian virtue of hope
has in our time grown so languid.
Where our fathers, peering into the future,
saw gleams of gold,
we see only the mist . . .

—C. S. Lewis

Dear Christina, Lisa, and Virginia,

We Christians are not the only ones who have high hopes. From the dawn of recorded history, people have cherished the hope that their spirits might survive death. Hope for an afterlife was common to religion and philosophy alike and survives to this day, even among friends of yours who have no faith to support it.

For example, the survival of the soul is the keystone of spiritualism. I mentioned in an earlier letter that Sir Arthur Conan Doyle, who created the sophisticated sleuth Sherlock Holmes, attempted to communicate with the soul of his dead son, and failed.

Frankly, I haven't the slightest desire to have my soul survive. You and I are flesh and blood, as well as spirit. Those who assume that the survival of their disembodied souls is a tenet of Christianity are gravely mistaken. That hope is alien to the Christian faith. Instead, our hope is expressed in the Apostles' Creed: *I believe in the resurrection of the body, and life everlasting*. Christians, whether confident or timid, do not believe that eternal life is mere *survival*, nor do they believe that they will live eternally as separated spirits. Rather, you will each exist as complete creatures, body and soul, in a whole new life of unimaginable splendor.

Before you were born, the American novelist William Faulkner received the Nobel Prize for literature. At the time, the world was threatened by nuclear annihilation, and humankind's hope had worn thin. In a remarkable acceptance speech, Faulkner expressed his conviction that humankind would not only survive, but prevail. In eternal terms, that is precisely the hope of Christians, and it is based squarely on the victory of Jesus over death. Christ did not simply survive death; he prevailed over it and, in body and spirit, assumed new life. Jesus was the first-born of the New Creation, inaugurating the Kingdom of God, of which we are now citizens, enjoying the promise of new life.

In eternity, you and I will be the same, yet different—just as Jesus was himself, yet somehow altered and enhanced following his Resurrection. All of the apostles were witnesses of his Resurrection, which became the cornerstone of their faith. Others witnessed the risen Christ as well, but none of his friends recognized him immediately. When Mary met him at the open tomb, she thought Jesus was a stranger, and established his identity only after he spoke to her (see John 20:14). The two companions Jesus joined on the road to Emmaus conversed with him all day, but failed to grasp his identity until he broke bread with them at supper (see Luke 24:13). The apostle Thomas doubted the Resurrection until Jesus appeared and invited him to put his fingers in the place of the wounds of his crucifixion (see John 11:27).

Skeptics suggest that the alteration in Jesus' appearance reveals that he was an imposter. But that begs the question. Eventually, everyone who had known him before his death was convinced that he was the risen Lord, and they were awed. Jesus had not just returned to life as he had been before his death; he had *changed.* He had not merely survived an ordeal—he was glorified.

You are heirs of the same hope: that you who believe in him will be not only restored as your present selves, but transformed into new and better creatures. When Jesus promised his crucified companion, "Today you will be with me in paradise" (Luke 23:43), it was no idle promise of spiritual survival, but of eternal joy.

Resisting Paradise

As hopeful as this prospect sounds, you will understand why some Christians are uncomfortable with it. For starters, many of us don't especially care for our bodies. Bodies get old and sick, and most aren't as tall and sleek as we wish them to be. Of course, the three of you are attractive women, but each of you has carried chronic ailments since childhood. Why would you want to drag these imperfect carcasses along into eternity?

The simple answer is that we can't get along without them. We are not pure spirits; our souls are hapless without our senses to acquire information and arms and legs to move us about. Our minds are empty without brains to process our thoughts. We are not angels, nor were we meant to be. Our bodies are a gift, not a curse. (They are not even sinful; we sin with our minds.)

Jesus himself did not shrug off his body when he conquered death. In eternity he is—like us—fully human. If that is the eternal state he has chosen for himself, then having a body can't be all that bad.

There is yet another awkwardness about believing in the resurrection of the body. Educated Christians have persuaded themselves that heaven is not a place, but a state of being. But bodily resurrection forces us back into the unsophisticated and necessary conclusion that heaven must be a place after all; still, it is clearly nowhere in space that we have explored.

In art school, Lisa, you studied an array of fanciful Renaissance paintings of the risen Christ ascending like a hot-air balloon into heaven. But now, long after persuading yourself that heaven is not "up there," you are back to contemplating Jesus rising into a cloud and disappearing—to *where* exactly it is impossible to imagine.

Hopeful Christians cannot wriggle out of this enigma. The risen Christ was real and corporeal. There were simply too many witnesses and too many occasions when the resurrected Jesus appeared to his friends for anyone to dismiss the experience as mass hallucination. But he remained on earth only six weeks, then clearly disappeared. Jesus justified his departure by saying that he was "going away to prepare a place for you . . . to welcome you into my own home, so that you may be where I am" (John 14: 2–3). By Luke's account, Jesus was then "lifted up before their eyes till a cloud hid him from their sight" (Acts 1:9).

How can confident Christians, free of embarrassment, admit to their neighbors that they place their hope in a God-man who flies in the air like Superman? With the same confidence that they hold that Jesus also walked on water! Christ not only commanded nature (as God had done ever since he created it); he *changed* it. He is the author of a New Creation which never dies and to which you belong.

As for the Ascension itself, Jesus had to leave to prepare our way, and he departed intact—body and spirit. The Evangelists do not belabor the point. Jesus was somehow glorified and disappeared from their view. What they are at pains to avoid implying is that Jesus was only a spirit or apparition all along. That would be to deny his Resurrection—and yours and mine.

Life as New Creatures

Once you absorb the significance of Jesus' Resurrection for your own future, you are at liberty to speculate about the nature of the New Creation to which you belong.

Unfortunately, there is not much to go on. We must obtain all our clues from the risen Christ himself. In his new form, he appeared and disappeared at will, passing through locked doors like a ghost. Yet, he insisted that he was not a spirit, and dined with his friends on fish.

Although he welcomed Thomas's touch to prove that he was corporeal, in some sense the risen Christ resisted physical contact. For example, in one instance, he said, "No! Do not hold me now. I have not yet gone up to the Father" (John 20:17). Demonstrably, Jesus is still human and physical, but he is a new man, belonging to a new nature that is not wholly comfortable with the old nature that you and I still inhabit.

Jesus confounds our old notions of immortality. He did not *escape* from the physical world as some kind of free spirit. Rather, he constituted a new kind of person consistent with the old. Instead of dispensing with his physical universe at the end of time, God has remade it to suit resurrected men and women.

Predictably, critics of Christian hope consider such speculation to be mere contrivance. What they prefer is simple religion or no religion at all. Alas, our faith is not simple. It is full of paradox: a God who is one, yet three; a Christ who is at once God and man; men and women who are both body and spirit. Moreover, ours is a religion that acknowledges both good and evil, providence and accident, comedy and tragedy. If it is a mysterious faith, it is at least not simplistic or boring. It does not gloss over reality. Confident Christians love God not because their Creator and Redeemer is predictable, but because he is full of surprises, all of which are good news for you.

The Evangelists report that before he raised his close friend Lazarus from the dead, Jesus wept (see John 11:33). Being human, it was only predictable that Jesus would display human emotion, but perhaps his tears meant more than that. At that moment all Jesus was prepared to do was to restore his friend to the life he had enjoyed *before,* in suburban Bethany with his sisters, Mary and Martha.

Of course Lazarus's restoration to life was a miracle, but it meant only that he must pick up where he left off, grow old, and eventually die like everyone else. Jesus, in this instance, stopped the relentless cycle of death, but his friend was not reborn to *new* and eternal life. It would take Jesus' own death to accomplish that—for himself, for Lazarus, and for you.

Once risen, Jesus was seen speaking with two of the ancient dead, demonstrating that he was already raising up others to new life. The Evangelists relate that Jesus, in his new body, literally glowed. He was luminous, the way he appears at the beginning of the Book of Revelation. Saint Mark says that not only Jesus' face shone, but his clothing as well (see Mark 9:2). On occasions, when you are very pleased, I have remarked that you are "glowing"—and it's true. That's the way you will be eternally in the New Creation.

New Heaven, New Earth

C. S. Lewis suspects that you and I resist assimilating the resurrected Jesus into our faith because we are wedded to the notion of a universe that consists of only two floors: nature as we know it, and the world of pure spirit. Perhaps that is why we prefer an immortality that involves the spirit leaving the body behind and somehow making it on its own eternally.

But Jesus' new life after his Resurrection confounds that simple notion and forces us to rethink our notions of nature and heaven. As it is, we Christians are hard-pressed to imagine what kind of life a disembodied spirit might have in an undifferentiated, unconditioned super-nature. But there are indications that eternity is not at all like that. Angels, for instance, although they are pure spirits, move between eternity and time and have personalities and activities. They are creatures, unhampered by their lack of bodies.

But humans are, in fact, "hampered," and there is no intimation that we are to be converted into angels. Rather, we will be new men and new women. Lewis suggests that the example of the risen Christ forces us to consider that there is yet another floor between nature and spirit. From the point of view of the old human nature that Jesus commanded and changed, our new nature will be *super*natural as well as physical.

From God's point of view, heaven is the divine life. From your human perspective, heaven is your participation in that life. The place that Jesus went to prepare for you is where all redeemed human spirits, *still remaining physical as well as spiritual*, will enjoy that participation completely and eternally.

It should be no surprise to you that the afterlife is more complex than you once thought. We already know that in heaven there are "many mansions," and Roman Catholics have long posited a nonbiblical purgatory in the afterlife for those not yet ready for glory. Salvation consists not only of reconciling creatures to their Creator, but of reconciling bodies and spirits with one another—restoring the original integrity of human nature so that we will at last be "together." That reconciliation—that peace—is a fact of life in the New Creation.

Hints of Eternity

We get hints of the New Creation when we experience great art, music, and literature, as well as the splendors of nature and human love. Strictly speaking, none of these gifts is spiritual, yet each enables us, if briefly, to transcend the mundane and create a temporary truce between our bodies and our spirits. Christian mystics sometimes have been suspected of being insufficiently "spiritual," because they employ the imagery of rapture to describe their experience of God. Rather than dismiss mysticism out of hand as frustrated human sexuality, it makes better sense to regard the ecstasies you and I occasionally experience in this life as a foretaste of the bliss we will know in the New Creation.

Sexual love is at once the most desired and the most abused pleasure enjoyed by fallen humankind, but it is unfairly denigrated as purely physical. Psychologists reveal that sex is in our "heads," not our bodies! In the New Creation there will be no war between body and spirit. To contemplate the face of God for all eternity will not be an act of your intellects alone, but of your bodies and spirits functioning together as never before. You will be regenerate Eves. Lamentably, pleasure has gained a bad name in religion, but only a Puritan would hope for an eternity that was less than ecstatic.

To its credit, Islam posits a heaven which, if not exactly a New Creation, consists of the very best features of the world you know. The Moslem heaven is a paradise—an eternal oasis for the faithful voyager who has crossed the desert of this life. It is unabashedly sensuous, and even sensual. Even as an Eden of the mind as well as the body, however, it falls short of the New Creation. Faithful Moslems do not expect to be transformed, but only to survive, and their bliss will consist of gifts from their Creator rather than union with him.

By contrast with Christianity and Islam, Judaism is altogether ambivalent about the afterlife. In Jesus' time, Jews hoped at most to attain a state of suspended animation after death. Today, there is no consensus among Jews about life after death, let alone a regenerate human nature and a New Creation.

The great Eastern religions offer their adherents even less hope. Buddhism, for instance, teaches that the essential nature of life is suffering, and that the human spirit is imprisoned in the body. The eternity they envision consists not of a New Creation of regenerate men and women, but of the soul's unlikely escape from life as we know it. For Buddhism and Hinduism alike, salvation is essentially negative—shrugging off this mortal coil—and hope remains the refuge of the very few who manage to elude fate and break the endless chain of rebirth.

The Price of Hope

The major religions are great precisely because they possess and preserve insights into human existence that are consistent with the experience of generations of men and women across time and cultures, including our own. Great faiths do not bend with the wind or bow to fashion. Still, they are not equivalent in their tenets or their hopes. Christianity alone holds out a destiny that respects the generosity of God and the dignity of each individual human being, such that God's own Son became one of us to save us for an eternity of joy.

As confident Christians, you trust that you will rise with Christ to new life. Along with all humankind, you cherish great expectations, because your hopes have been raised by a God who saves you from yourselves and for himself. Not that these expectations are exclusive to Christians; God is not the prisoner of Christianity. Rather, God is the One who created all and is the hope of all.

Your hope, like your Christian faith, is a gift utterly unearned. It is neither a bonus nor extra credit, but rather salvation from hopelessness and an expression of God's love for you. As the old spiritual proclaims:

> *I once was lost*
> *but now am found,*
> *was blind, but now I see.*

That spiritual expresses wisdom. Whenever you feel lost or blind, do not try to find God. He has already found you. In your hope you will regain sight.

Although we are loath to admit it, most Christians suspect that our Creator went overboard by sending his Son to the cross; they wonder whether God couldn't have accomplished our redemption less dramatically. That is because we think of ourselves as pretty decent persons at heart, not as sinners. We wonder why Jesus had to go to so much trouble for us. Surely we can't be so bad as to require such a drastic remedy. A little self-improvement, perhaps, an occasional touch-up, self-applied of course—but not a total makeover!

Atonement

But there are plenty of people who think otherwise. They know they need saving, because they have hit bottom, so far down in life's dregs that the only way to look is up. Poverty, chronic illness, marital and professional failure, and addiction bring people down to desperation. As a social worker, Christina, you deal with desperate people every day. You know that, as long as addicts regard themselves as mere *victims*, they cannot be saved. They will only despair, curse the world and their companions, and blame their Creator for their fates. In a final do-it-yourself confrontation with hopelessness, they may kill themselves.

Long before you were born, I handled a suicide hotline in Chicago. I was on call through the dark hours when hopeful people slept and desperate men and women lay awake contemplating putting an end to their misery. During my long, desultory conversations with prospective suicides, their chronic complaint was that they were victims. Few phoned for a helping hand; most only wanted to share with me their misery and righteous anger at their plight. Unfortunately, compassion is not enough to save people who refuse to take responsibility for their condition and accept a helping hand.

The reason Alcoholics Anonymous and similar twelve-step programs work is because their members admit they need salvation and cannot accomplish it themselves. Recovering alcoholics do not blame the bottle for their condition; rather, they blame themselves, but avoid wallowing in guilt—and they reach beyond themselves in hope. For recovering addicts, shame is no longer a deterrent to personal salvation, because every AA member acknowledges sharing the same condition. Salvation is the great equalizer. We all need it, none of us deserves it, and to obtain it, we need outside help.

Over the years, you and I have lived with alcoholics in our own family and have experienced firsthand how adept they are at self-deception. Two of my cousins literally died in the gutter from alcoholism, a dramatic illustration that denial ultimately fails. To break the cycle, alcoholics must admit their self-loathing condition, take responsibility for it, and acknowledge that they can't save themselves, that they must rely on fellow addicts and a Higher Power that is interested in their welfare and can do something about it.

At AA meetings, alcoholics confess their sins to fellow sinners and ask for help. The road of recovery is long. Indeed, even those who have not touched a drop of alcohol in decades refer to themselves as "recovering alcoholics," because they know that their need for salvation is ongoing.

Sinners

Two thousand years ago, the motives of people who flocked to John the Baptist at the River Jordan were strikingly similar to those who attend twelve-step programs today:

> *In due course John the Baptist arrived, preaching in the Judean desert: "You must change your hearts—for the kingdom of Heaven has arrived!" . . . Go and do something to show that your hearts are really changed"* (Matthew 3:1–2; 8).

God's promise to you is premised on the fact that we are all sinners. Repentance and confession are first steps toward the change of heart that prompts us to "do something" to open ourselves to the promise, becoming heirs to hope. Without repentance, we are closed to hope, because we refuse to acknowledge our common condition: alienation from a loving God. Just as the person who hasn't had a drink in a decade admits, "I am still an alcoholic," you and I must acknowledge that we are still sinners. Otherwise, we embrace our failings and have no hope.

When you were young, you were sometimes willful and quickly learned to manipulate your mother and me with affection. Before your time, I did the same with my parents. Left alone, young children would reenact *Lord of the Flies*, vandalize the world, and abandon one another. Even in our idealistic youth, seeking a more perfect world, we act as self-appointed heroes in our own life's drama. None of us is innocent.

With luck, you and I will not do much harm during our lives. God willing, on balance, we will do more good. But our basic motivation remains self-centered, and we will never be quite sure that our heroism is anything more than a sham. Nevertheless, we play it out, not especially admiring ourselves, but concerned that others approve of us and will validate our lives by love. In adolescence and early adulthood, we learn to put on masks to gain that approval, adjusting our ideas, ideals, and behavior to suit the company we happen to be in. That's human nature before the New Creation.

As we mature, each of us becomes a little god around whom the universe revolves, although we learn—to our dismay—that there is little we can do to bend the universe to our own will. Nor can we be certain of other people because they, too, wear masks and have their own agendas. They occupy the center of their own individual universes, in which we are but satellites. In moments of truth, we all realize that we're playing the same game of mutual and self-deception.

"They Know Not What They Do"

Fooling ourselves about ourselves is the foundation of human sinfulness, and it leads to the real evils that destroy others and even ourselves. Self-deception too easily translates into self-justification, whereby we write off our sins of commission and omission as only minor footnotes in otherwise blameless lives. When we unwittingly fail others or ignore their needs, we are inclined to pardon ourselves while blaming our victims for their predicaments. In such a world of self-forgiveness, what need is there for the Son of God to die on the cross for us?

Revealingly, the dying Jesus forgave his tormentors with the prayer, "Father, forgive them, because they don't know what they are doing" (Luke 23:34). What can Christ's pardon mean? If his executioners were truly ignorant of the sin of torturing and murdering an innocent man, then theirs was no sin. Indeed, if they thought they were actually doing God's will by ridding the world of this pretender then, by rights, what they were doing was actually virtuous!

Apologist Homer Rogers explains that what required Jesus' forgiveness was his tormentors' *blindness*, because it was self-deception, the kind of blindness we all use as a defense against the truth about ourselves. Everyone connected to Jesus' death had a good excuse. Pilate was only being a good Roman bureaucrat; the Sanhedrin were keeping the faith pure; the Roman soldiers were being dutiful. No one bothered to think about the consequences of what they were doing, because they already knew they were honorable people.

They deceived themselves because they would not acknowledge that Jesus was better than they were. In the presence of goodness, people have only two options: to acknowledge another's moral superiority and seek to emulate it; or to resent that goodness and try to find its flaw. The reason Jesus' executioners were unwilling to crucify him as a common criminal was because they suspected he was not *common* at all. Jesus stood silent during his trial, never defending himself, never protesting his treatment, never once pleading for his life.

In an attempt to break Jesus' spirit and get him to plead like a common criminal, they derided him, spat on him, crowned him with thorns, beat him, slapped him, stripped him, made him carry his own cross, then mocked him with a placard that read "King of the Jews," and taunted him to prove his divinity by saving himself.

You know full well that ordinary people can act either beastly or heroically in harsh circumstances. During the Holocaust, for example, ordinary German conscripts from good Christian families committed hideous atrocities, justifying themselves because in their minds and hearts they had already demonized their victims, just as Jesus' tormentors had demonized him.

"I am right because you are wrong," is the perennial justification for evil. Jesus died because God's way of dealing with sin was not to resist, not to return sin for sin, but to overcome evil with good. The only thing that can bring you and me to a sense of our own sinfulness is the realization that we have caused the suffering of innocent persons. Only two strangers at the crucifixion realized the evil they were doing: the centurion and Pilate's wife (see Matthew 27:19; Luke 23:47). Each concluded that, of all the parties surrounding the cross, the only good man was the one nailed to it, and they had unwittingly helped put him there.

A Sense of Sin

Of course, there is a world of difference between *feeling* guilt and *being* guilty. Alone among God's creatures, we humans blush in embarrassment. We are more often embarrassed by our blunders and our appearance than by our sins. Using the wrong fork is not evil, nor is having a "bad hair day," but we blush nonetheless!

Humorists have a field day with Jewish mothers who have the knack of making their adult children feel guilty because of alleged inattention. Rabbi Harold Kushner wrote his book *How Good Do We Have to Be?* to help readers distinguish between guilt feelings and real guilt. When I reviewed the book in my newspaper column, I suggested that Kushner was possibly letting his guilt-ridden readers off too easily. The realistic answer to the question raised in his book's title is that we all have to be a lot better than we are no matter how we feel.

There is plenty of real guilt to go around, whether we feel it or not. You may wish to think the best about people, but no one can view the human situation and deny the evil that men and women cause one another though malevolence and carelessness. It is pointless to blame the world's violence and poverty on God when we are clearly their creators. God made the environment good; we dirty it. God does not have to tidy up his act; we need to clean up ours.

But, in fact, God *did* clean up our act for us; that was the point of Jesus' incarnation, life, death, and resurrection. That is the good news you and I share as Christians.

I don't believe you ever had this experience but, as a young child, I was taught by sincere Christians that my sins nailed Jesus to the cross. That pronouncement was meant to make me feel guilty and, occasionally, it did unnerve me, but I never really believed it. If God were really offended by my childish peccadilloes, he would have let me stew in my own juices; he wouldn't have bothered to send his Son to die for me. But he did.

God is not a Jewish mother. He sent his Son to save us not because of his own hurt feelings, but because he knows (better than we) the sorry situation we have placed ourselves in by playing God ourselves. We need saving all right—salvation from ourselves.

When I was a young child, Jesus' message from the cross applied to me: "Forgive David because he doesn't know what he is doing." But as I got older and more aware of my self-centeredness, I have needed Jesus to say: "Father, forgive David because he knows perfectly well what he is doing!" Childish shame was no longer sufficient to bring me to heel; I needed saving!

It is through the suffering of the innocent—Jesus the most prominent among them—that we awake to a sense of our sin, our real guilt, and our need of reconciliation. If Jesus' death on a cross sometimes seems too dramatic a gesture to drive home the point, it is at least effective.

God's Point of View

Intelligent as you are, you will never understand salvation if you start from your own perspective, because your sins seem too trivial to merit God's concern. But from God's point of view, it makes perfect sense that the Creator would want to restore integrity to the creation he once called "good" by making it good once again. We humans are the creatures he made in his own image, but we have been too zealous to prove to ourselves that likeness by asserting our independence from the outset, each of us acting like a little god in his or her own universe. When creatures originally alienated their Creator, God acknowledged the breach, then progressively moved to repair the separation. That is the story of our salvation revealed in the Bible.

The technical term for what Jesus accomplished is *atonement*. If you recall, your Sunday school teachers dismembered the word to reveal its meaning: *at-one-ment*. In short, healing the wound, getting us back at one with God the way things were intended to be—and will be fully in the New Creation.

But if Jesus was successful in atonement, why is there still sin? Because you and I retain our independence. The mere availability of grace and forgiveness, and the reality of the New Creation, do not require us to accept them. You and I can, each of us, still keep playing God. Revealingly, none of us chooses to play the way the Son of God actually did: from a cross.

The Prodigal Son's father was always ready to forgive him and welcome him home, but the son had to make the decision to return. He could not make that decision until he acknowledged how miserable and alone he was, and was prepared to take responsibility for his situation.

Having acknowledged our faults, it only follows that you and I must forgive others theirs. Then a great burden—of which we were formerly unaware—will be lifted from us, and the Spirit of God who dwells in us finally will have some room to work. That work is to affirm us as citizens of the New Creation, where at last we will see life, and ourselves, from *God's* point of view.

Faithfully,

Your father

Part III

Love

And now abideth faith, hope, love,
these three;
But the greatest of them is love.

—1 Corinthians 13:13

Chapter 7

Keep the Rules

> Morality did not begin by one man saying to another,
> "I will not hit you if you do not hit me";
> there is no trace of such a transaction.
> There is a trace of both men having said,
> "We must not hit each other in the holy place."
> They gained their morality by guarding their religion.
>
> —G. K. Chesterton

Dear Christina, Lisa, and Virginia,

Although you possess faith in God and hope for your eternal future, you must still make your way through this life with confidence. In life's journey, you, like other men and women, will be guided by law and conscience. Because you are Christians, you will also follow the dictates of love. But you must first obey the rules.

Love is the distinguishing characteristic of Christ's followers; still, no human society has ever functioned on love's imperatives alone. For that, you and I must await the fulfillment of the New Creation. Meanwhile, you wend your way through life's labyrinth by obeying the dictates of law and conscience. Conscience is the internal compass that helps steer moral minimalists to do more—to act fairly, compassionately, and generously. Despite Jiminy Cricket's reassurances to Pinocchio about the virtue of truth-telling, however, conscience is not an infallible guide. Even with the best of intentions, you can blunder by following this crude internal compass. Thus, parents and teachers *inform* children's consciences by teaching and example.

Of course, parents want more for their children than to keep them law-abiding. Your mother and I are delighted that we have never been obliged to bail you out of jail but, as parents do, we tried to teach you to be reliable, honest, fair, and compassionate. To be sure, you have fared better than many other Americans, over a million of whom are in federal and state prisons. Many more men and women are in city and county jails, and tens of thousands of children are in detention homes.

Seventeenth-century essayist John Ray noted that "in a thousand pounds of law there is not an ounce of love," decrying the harsh justice of his day. Still, law remains the firm foundation of civilization. Without it, anarchy reigns, love is stifled, and we all become candidates for victimization.

Although God is motivated solely by love, it is noteworthy that he based his covenant with the chosen people on law, binding them to a contract that specified mutual obligations of fidelity. By contrast, our civil society is a compact among peoples that merely protects us from one another and promotes our general welfare. That there are so very many laws demonstrates how difficult it is for society to contain its members' savagery, greed, and indifference, and serve the common weal.

God's law is not only better motivated, but it is simpler than human law. At last count, the state of Florida alone had 28,750 statutes on its books to regulate the behavior of its citizens. Beyond that, the citizens of Florida—and any state—are bound by international, federal, and local laws as well. In the planned community where your mother and I live and you grew up, families voluntarily bind themselves to scores of additional covenants to ensure neighborliness. You may remember when a new neighbor of ours installed a blue rural mailbox (instead of the approved black model), and was hailed into county court and fined. Well, black mailboxes are still the law!

Great Expectations

God's laws, given to us by Moses some thirty-two centuries ago, are not only simpler but less numerous than civil laws. There are but ten of them, and they can be further condensed to two: to love God and to obey the Golden Rule.

Although the Mosaic law includes proscriptions of murder, theft, adultery, and perjury that have since been incorporated in our civil law, God established other expectations that do not easily translate into statute. The command to honor one's parents, for example, is more of a tribal and cultural expectation than a legal one. Similarly, the condemnation of covetousness is a brake on ambition and passion rather than on overt action. When a born-again Christian president of the United States, Jimmy Carter, confessed that he sometimes lusted in his heart, he transgressed no civil statute and incurred no fine—but he clearly felt that he had failed God's expectations of him.

As to the three remaining Mosaic commandments, two call for honoring God and the third requires observance of the Sabbath. It is true that in the not-so-distant past, states and localities enforced "blue" laws prohibiting the sale of liquor and the opening of stores and theaters on Sunday. The Christian lawmakers had good intentions, but even Sunday closing laws could not keep the Sabbath sacred or ensure that citizens kept their minds on God.

So only four of the Ten Commandments proscribe behavior that can be punished by society; the others define the attitudes a faithful man or woman should take toward God and neighbor. These are less prohibitions than positive obligations.

It is worth recalling that God gave but a single law to the first man and woman, and they foolishly transgressed it by competing with him. In the story of the flood, God attempted once again to befriend his creatures and to sustain them, signing his covenant with a rainbow. Then he chose Abraham, delivered his descendants from slavery, made them a gift of the promised land, and dictated through Moses the faithfulness he expected in return. It was the only time in history when God himself acted as legislator for an entire nation.

God's expectations are contained in the first five books of the Bible, known as the *Torah*, a word that means "instruction." Unlike the judgments of kings, emperors, and dictators, God's demands are not arbitrary and self-serving. Instead, they are moral: they are good for the people God loves, which includes all of us.

The Promised Land

A unique characteristic of God's law is that it is tied to the promised land. Its provisions are similar to those found in a lease, with God the owner and the Israelites his leaseholders: "The land is mine and you are . . . my tenants" (Leviticus 25:23). For the Jews, unlike other peoples before and since, law came with the gift of land. Their covenant was in the form of a lease that, while permanent, could be suspended for bad tenant behavior.

Each of you has signed leases, so you know that such contracts are serious, that you must pay your rent on time. The only "rent" the Jews had to pay, however, was fidelity, and they often fell behind on payment. The history of the Jews can be read as the chronicle of their possession and repossession of the promised land, and their eviction from it.

A lingering, but shrinking, group of biblical scholars contend that Moses is a fictitious character and that the Mosaic law was fabricated by priests after the Babylonian exile. Against this skepticism, Paul Johnson, in his book titled *A History of the Jews*, argues that Moses is beyond the power of the human mind to invent, and that his strength leaps off the printed page now, even as it then swayed the unruly people wandering in the Sinai Desert on their way to the land of milk and honey.

Today you might consider Moses a utopian engineer, because he succeeded in translating divine idealism into practical governance. If God was ruler, judge, and legislator for a nation, then Moses was his brilliant chancellor and effective prime minister. Every aspect, public and private, of Israelite life was driven by this man whom Johnson calls a "totalitarian of the spirit."

When the Jews were delivered from bondage in Egypt, you might have expected them to borrow their sense of law from that land of their captivity. But in Egypt, a static society, law consisted only of the whim of the pharaoh, who was revered as a god-king. Because Egyptian law was only personal, casual, and mutable, it was not committed to writing, and it lacked permanence and portability. But when Moses carved God's commandments in stone, he dramatized their permanence and distanced Jewish law from the fickle fiat of the pharaohs.

The essence of the Mosaic law probably dates from 1250 B.C. While unique as a code, it echoed a long-standing Mesopotamian tradition that valued the permanence of written law. The patriarch Abraham himself was probably aware of the Code of Ur Nammu, dating from 2050 B.C., as well as the property laws of the ancient kingdom of Eshnuna. Moses, who studied law in the court of the pharaoh, surely knew of the Code of Hammurabi, dating from 1728–1686 B.C.

To dignify their laws, Mesopotamian rulers claimed they were divinely inspired, but acknowledged themselves to be their human authors. By contrast, Moses insisted that he was only a messenger—that God alone wrote the law and made his covenant with the Jews. Subsequently, no Israelite king or prophet presumed to tamper with the law which, from the outset, made no distinction between the religious or secular. Civil, moral, and criminal law are indistinguishable for the Jews. Crimes are sins; sins are crimes; and it is God who indicts and convicts—no mere human judge can pardon. In Jewish law, even if a thief restores stolen goods, his victim's forgiveness is insufficient because God seeks restitution as well.

An Eye for an Eye

In other legal systems in the ancient world, a husband might occasionally pardon his wife and her lover of the crime of adultery, but Mosaic code insisted that the adulterous couple be executed because God, too, was offended. Adultery was not only a crime against a human being, but it was a sin against the Creator. Underlying this severity was the Israelites' acknowledgment that they *belonged* to God in the most radical way. He was their God, but they were his people.

The Mosaic code's consistency, oddly enough, made it democratic. The rich could not buy their way out of its punishments nor retain wily lawyers to plea-bargain their way to lighter sentences. To be sure, God's law made distinctions regarding lesser or unintentional offenses. If, for example, a man killed another when he intended only to injure him, he was not expected to pay for his offense with his own life. In such cases, the Mosaic code called for strict compensation—"eye for eye, tooth for tooth, hand for hand, foot for foot" (Exodus 21:22). Later, of course, Jesus would call for us Christians to respond to injury with love. But in the ancient world, where people murdered one another on the slightest provocation, the rule of "eye-for-eye" proved to be a great leap forward in civilized behavior.

Because the God of Israel was recognized as Creator of all living things, the law of Israel attached extraordinary significance to life. Man and woman, created in God's own image, occupied sacred lives. Accordingly, a murderer was considered to have destroyed God's own likeness in another person, so his own life was forfeit. Ironically, the Old Testament insistence on the death penalty underscored the Jews' reverence for life.

The Mosaic law, however, was less harsh than the codes of surrounding nations in dealing with offenses against mere property—typically calling for restitution and a financial penalty. It forbade punishing a miscreant's family for his crimes. Whereas other ancient cultures permitted facial mutilation, castration, impalement, and flogging to death, Jewish law limited physical punishment to forty lashes out of respect for the human body God had given the criminal.

Although other societies agreed on the most serious offenses that merited judgment, nowhere else in antiquity is there such a comprehensive statement of duties and obligations toward God and humans as contained in the Mosaic law. Inevitably, the implications of each commandment in time became laws themselves, and the original Decalogue was elaborated into rules governing a Jew's every waking moment. Even before Jesus' entry into history, Judaic scholars proclaimed 613 commandments, including 248 obligations and 365 prohibitions. The original Ten Commandments had expanded more than sixty times over!

Sex, Diet, and Circumcision

Compared to their neighbors, the Jews took a strict attitude toward sex. Whereas Ugaritic law allowed fornication, adultery, bestiality, and incest, and Egyptian society permitted the marriage of close relatives, Jewish law proscribed all sexual irregularities as unclean in God's sight. Jewish dietary law was equally strict. Prohibitions reflected Egyptian practice and had some scientific basis. Even today, Jews shun shellfish and pork, which are susceptible to bacterial contamination; whereas pious Egyptians in ancient times shunned seafood altogether. Jewish dietary law favored the flesh of "clean" animals, principally those who were vegetarian, cloven-footed, and ruminant. Hunting wild animals for food was forbidden because it was risky. The eating of camel meat was banned because that animal had better uses for the Jews alive than dead.

Although male circumcision was customary among Egyptians, Edomites, Moabites, and Ammonites, the Israelites attached transcendent importance to the ritual. The Bible notes that circumcision was performed by the patriarch Abraham on his son as part of the original covenant (see Acts 7:8). In the ancient societies that practiced it, circumcision was an initiation rite for marriage, routinely performed when a boy reached adolescence. But Mosaic law called for the ritual removal of the foreskin on the eighth day after *birth*, and Moses' own son was circumcised by his mother even earlier. Henceforth, for the chosen people, the practice no longer merely signaled the onset of puberty, but became the sign of the covenant itself, borne by every Jewish male. Its significance was obvious, making God's mark on the organ that perpetuated the people of God.

Of course, the legal institution of the Sabbath had its practical value as a periodic day of rest for slaves and beasts of burden, as well as for Israelite workers. But Israel made the Sabbath distinctive as a holy day on which they reflected that they were a chosen people.

The sojourners to whom Moses delivered God's law were, by the standards of many of their Middle Eastern neighbors, a primitive and superstitious people, burdened by taboos and swayed by magic. Just as Jesus later worked miracles in part to attract attention to his preaching, Moses and the early Israelite prophets were prompted to practice wizardry to attract this credulous people to law, faith, and fidelity.

The Power of Monotheism

But magic was only for show. The Jews' fundamental faith in one all-powerful God precluded belief in any competing sources of power in the universe. Moreover, God's covenant persuaded the Jews that his law was perpetual and immutable, and that their Creator was neither selfish nor whimsical, as pagan deities were. Jewish monotheism was utterly revolutionary in the ancient world, accounting for the persistence of these people when more powerful and sophisticated nations disappeared altogether from history. God—the *only* God—was on their side and could be trusted to keep his end of the covenant if they would uphold theirs.

Although it was considered to be a grave national tragedy, the Babylonian exile in the sixth century B.C. disciplined ordinary Jews, for the first time, in the daily, detailed practice of their law. To preserve the identity of the nation in exile, the laws were copied, studied, read aloud, and memorized. The Sabbath became the focus of the Jewish week in exile, and a year-round progression of ritual observances was celebrated. Israel in exile could pretend no longer to political cohesion, but each individual remained bound by God's law:

> *These commandments that I give you today are to be upon your hearts. Impress them on your children. Talk about them when you sit at home and when you walk along the road, when you lie down and when you get up. Tie them as symbols on your hands and bind them on your foreheads. Write them on the doorframes of your houses and on your gates* (Deuteronomy 6:6–9).

In exile, the Jews retained national solidarity by voluntarily submitting to a law that lacked police and courts to enforce it. Nothing like the cohesion of the Jews has been duplicated by other peoples before or since. Other emigres retain their culture for a time but eventually are drawn into the ethnic melting pot and become amalgamated into their host culture. But the Jews' sense of divine election, enforced by a law that dictated the details of their lives, served to preserve their uniqueness and exclusivity.

Attempts at Revisionism

Upon their return from the Babylonian captivity, many sophisticated Jews found their nation's moral exclusivity to be stifling. They had lived away from home and sensed that they were isolated from a grander world that admired Greek culture. Accordingly, reformers sought to reconcile Jewish faith with Greek civilization by reducing God's rigorous law to its ethical core, which even the Greeks and Romans might respect. At the time, it seemed to be the sophisticated thing to do.

But in 167 B.C. the Selucid monarch Antiochus Epiphanes, in a move to suppress Jewish exclusivity in the lands under his sway, replaced Mosaic law with his purely secular law and converted the Temple in Jerusalem into a shrine dedicated to pagan deities as well as to the God of the Jews. Jewish traditionalists revolted, drove the Selucids out of Jerusalem, and rededicated the Temple to the God of the covenant in 164 B.C.

By 142 B.C. Israel was once again politically independent after 440 years. Orthodox Judaism held sway, supported by a new national system of religious schools designed specifically to uphold Jewish law against pagan culture. It was in these schools that the written Mosaic law began to be augmented by Oral Law—commentary that permitted the original code to adapt to changing conditions.

The development of Oral Law was denounced by the Sadducees, who accepted only the written biblical code, but it was embraced by the Pharisees. By the time of Jesus, this issue, as well as the priority of Temple worship, had come to a boil and explains why he was questioned so sharply about his views of the law. Each religious party wanted to know which side Jesus was on. But there were other disputing parties as well. One, led by Shammai the Elder (c. 50 B.C.–c. A.D. 30) was rigorist, especially on issues of diet and hygiene, insisting that the essence of the Mosaic law was in its details.

Against this severity, which effectively denied piety to the poor and uneducated, stood the school of Hillel the Elder. Paul Johnson claims that Jesus embraced Hillel's school of thought, which emphasized behavior in the *spirit* (rather than the letter) of the Torah, arguing that if one acted with the right attitude, the details would take care of themselves.

Jesus and the Law

Jesus, who may have sat as one of Hillel's many students in the Temple, took the master's teaching to its logical conclusions, arguing that God's law was made for humans, not humans for the law. Provisions of the law and temple worship must not be allowed to stand between human beings and their Creator. Of course, living in the spirit of the law could be more demanding than living by its letter! For example, Jesus' prohibition of divorce exceeded the requirements of the most rigorist legal interpreters of his day, who allowed a man to cast away an adulterous wife.

Jesus was considered a traitor to the law for preaching that salvation comes by way of faith, hope, and love rather than by righteous adherence to the law's letter. According to Jesus, it is God's grace that prompts the believer to respect God's law. Therefore, even the poorest, least educated, and most flawed men and women can enjoy a direct relationship with their Creator. According to Jesus, no one *wins* God's favor by his or her own efforts, but can only *accept* God's promise gratefully. All of us are transgressors, but grace overcomes sin. The key to salvation is not meticulous obedience to the law; rather, it is the human being's loving response to a faithful

Creator. The law does not save, nor do we save ourselves by adherence to the law. Rather, it is God who saves.

It can be argued that Jesus' teachings so distanced him from orthodox Judaism that he ceased to be a Jew and started a new religion. But it is impossible to conceive of the Savior entering history except as a Jew, as one of the chosen people bound by a covenant with the one God. Had such an extraordinary person been born in a pagan civilization—in ancient Greece or Rome—he might have been admired as a philosopher, but not as redeemer. As it was, the Son of God emerged from the people of God.

Judaism is not speculative, but legalistic. It concentrates on human behavior and leaves the rest to God. But Jesus had much to say about matters beyond behavior. He spoke of death, judgment, and the afterlife, and he extended God's promise to everyone—to Samaritans and sinners, and to Gentiles as well as pious Jews. In full realization of how he was subverting strict legalism, Jesus supported his teaching with compassionate miracles. And for as long as possible, he kept the new radical ethics of the Sermon on the Mount and his identity as the Son of God between himself and his closest followers.

Although the Pharisees appear frequently in the Gospels as Jesus' antagonists, they were probably the party least threatened by his teachings, since they supported development of a flexible Oral Law. But the Sadducees and followers of Shammai would have seen Jesus as a threat. Although no evidence was brought against Jesus at his trial, his silence in the face of trumped-up charges was interpreted as assent to the allegations of his accusers. Under strict Jewish law, Jesus was liable to be stoned to death for his religious claim to be the Messiah, but it was more convenient to deliver him to the Roman authorities to be executed as a potential political threat.

From Law to Faith, from Jew to Gentile

Jesus' disciples understood his death and resurrection to herald a New Covenant, or New Testament. But at the outset, the original apostles were still so attached to their Jewish roots that they did little more than attempt to convince their fellow Jews that they had only made a grave mistake in delivering up Jesus for execution. They protested to little avail, however; as a nation, the Jews successfully resisted the missionary efforts of the infant church.

It was left to Paul of Tarsus, a Diaspora Jew (living outside Israel) with Galilean roots, to grasp the radical nature of this new faith and deliver it to the world. Some critics contend that Paul "invented" Christianity and that Jesus himself would not recognize the apostle's confection. But if you read Paul's letters, you will be persuaded that this highly educated Pharisee grasped the momentous implications of Jesus' life, death, and resurrection—as no former fisherman or tax collector could—and possessed the power to persuade others, including his fellow apostles.

Paul grasped that Jesus' prophesy of a New Covenant had already come into existence through his suffering for sin and his conquest of death. This New Covenant was available to everyone who has faith in it. The moral value of the Mosaic law remains, but law-keeping alone is insufficient for salvation. In fact, the law had become a diversion and an idol, so revered by the chosen people that it had taken the place of God.

Of course, faithfulness to God is required in the New Covenant, but our fidelity consists of more than going through the motions of law-abiding. Rather, it is our loving response to a faithful God—a response impossible without God's grace. God's plan has changed, Paul insisted. Grace no longer comes through the law, but through Jesus, who has superseded the law. The God of Israel is the God of all; his grace and salvation are now available to everyone who believes and enters into the New Covenant. Your very humanity—and mine—makes us eligible for faith and grace. Now, because of Jesus, *all* people are chosen people:

> *In this new man of God's design, there is no distinction between Greek and Hebrew, Jew or Gentile, foreigner or savage, slave or free man. Christ is all that matters, for Christ lives in them all* (Colossians 3:11).

Whereas pagan reformers had sought unsuccessfully to impose secularism on the Jews, Paul embraced the entire Jewish experience of God's revelation and extended it to the Gentiles. No longer was the letter of the law to be used as an arrogant weapon against the poor, the ignorant, the despised, and sinners, for these were the very persons Jesus had come to save. Paul now was free to carry forgiveness and hope to those who had never heard of the Mosaic law but had lived heretofore only by secular law and their consciences.

Not surprisingly, the world welcomed this ancient faith now unburdened of its rigid restrictions. Here was the radically democratic promise that the God of the Jews would make straight the crooked ways for everyone—enriching the poor, strengthening the weak, forgiving the sinner, preferring the simple to the wise, and uplifting the lowly. Here now was the promise to everyone—whatever his or her station in life—of eternal joy!

The Continuing Function of the Law

Paul made clear that the New Covenant does not nullify the law, but transcends it. Writing to the Gentiles, he pointed to the law as the standard of civilized group behavior, and told the converts to strive to keep the commandments:

> *Are we then undermining the law by this insistence on faith? Not a bit of it! We put the law in its proper place* (Romans 3:31).

In the New Covenant, Christ confirmed the promises made in the old covenant that was sealed by the law:

> *The law itself is holy, and the commandment is holy, fair and good* (Romans 7:12).

Nevertheless, Paul argued, the law alone is inadequate for salvation. Law condemned the transgressor but, alone, it could not redeem the righteous. Paul was proud to be a Jew, but recognized no advantage for the Gentiles to bind themselves to the law's dictates in order to profit from Christ's victory over death. All the richness of God's revelation to the Jews were henceforth available to the Christian convert.

Because Paul believed that Christ would soon return to end history and inaugurate the Kingdom of God, he did not bother to ponder why God made one covenant only to cancel it with another. It was enough for Paul to note that all of God's promises had been fulfilled in Christ.

By the time the Gospels were composed (some forty to seventy years after Jesus' death), Christianity's breach with Judaism had become irreversible. That may explain why the Evangelists were at pains to underscore Jesus' repudiation of the law. For example, when Mark quoted Jesus as affirming that people are morally defiled by their behavior rather than by their diet, the Evangelist turned it into a repudiation of kosher food. The Evangelist John recorded Jesus as condemning his Jewish listeners as children of Satan (see chapter 8), and consistently had Jesus contrasting the law that came from Moses with the grace and peace that come from God.

Matthew had Jesus in his Sermon on the Mount distinguish between what the Jews "have heard" (from Moses) and what "I say to you" (Matthew 5:21).

Luke, by contrast, downplayed these antilaw statements of Jesus. Indeed, all the Gospels present Jesus as honoring the law in his personal life, worshiping on the Sabbath, sacrificing in the Temple, and observing holy days and Passover. Revealingly, Jesus' followers continued to observe the Jewish Sabbath following his death, even postponing their visit to his tomb until Sunday, which in time became the Sabbath of the New Covenant.

If, on your early reading, the Gospels appear to be argumentative, it is because they accurately reflect how the sense of the law was developed through debate. If the Gospels appear to you to be occasionally anti-Semitic, it is only because today we assume argument to be hostile when, in Jesus' time, it was the approved way to get at the truth. A millennium and a half later, when Martin Luther heralded the Reformation by nailing his theological challenges on the cathedral door, he did not intend to start a fight, but only to open a debate.

Simple Law, Complicated Faith

As onerous as legalism became in Judaism, Christianity added complications of a different sort to your faith and mine. The simple genius of Jewish faith was monotheism. Ironically, more than anything else, it was the Jews' belief in one God that made Christianity repellant to them. We Christians believe that Jesus is both God and man, whereas the Jews adhere to an utter distinction between the human and the divine. On this issue alone, if Jesus is indeed God, Judaism was in error; if Jesus is not God, then Christianity is pointless.

From the outset, Christianity grappled with theological mysteries that did not distract Judaism—grace, Redemption, and the kingdom among them. At the same time, Christianity annexed everything else from Judaism—the Bible, the Sabbath, prayer and sacrifice, ritual, psalms, hymns, the priesthood, and even the synagogue and Temple (combined into the Church). If we Gentile Christians were not required to convert to Judaism, we nevertheless inherited all of its advantages and are richer for the fact.

The Jews, of course, have survived, and so has the Mosaic law with greater elaboration of the Oral Law than St. Paul ever confronted. Custom, too, has passed into Judaic law over the past two millennia. In *The Jewish Book of Why*, scholar Alfred J. Kolatch acknowledges that if a Jew of the generation of Moses or Solomon or Judas Maccabeus were to visit Jewry in our time, he would be bewildered by its practices.

Moses himself would wonder at the contemporary use of prayer shawls, girdles, and skullcaps, the foods served at *seders*, and many stories and songs of more recent origin. The prophets would be stunned by the proliferation of laws concerning conduct on the Sabbath, and the *yarmulkes* worn by men on the streets of modern Israel, fastened to their heads with ladies' bobby pins or hair clips. Moses might wonder how that practice squares with the commandment:

> *A woman must not wear men's clothing, nor a man wear women's clothing, for the Lord your God detests anyone who does this* (Deuteronomy 22:5).

Kolatch, a Jew, explains by quoting from the *Talmud*:

> *When you come to a town, follow its customs, for when Moses went up to heaven he refrained from food for 40 days and 40 nights. And when the angels came down to visit Abraham, they partook of his meal, each one submitting to the custom of the place* (Baba Metzia 86b).

If angels can bend the law to coincide with custom, so can the faithful Jew. It only illustrates what Jesus taught himself: that the law is made for humans; humans were not made for the law.

Law and the Confident Christian

The abiding motivation of Christians is love. Unfortunately, as generations of lovers attest, love is often blind. Although it ever seeks the good of another, love is, by nature, indiscriminate, overflowing, and unregulated. While love is always well intentioned, it does not necessarily know its appropriate object or expression. Alas, the world must turn on law as well as on love! Because lovers will sacrifice their life to save another's in a fire, such acts of generosity do not preclude the necessity of fire regulations.

Love without law and conscience is chaotic. That Christians are drawn into politics and law enforcement attests to our belief that good laws undergird a just society. In daily life, you do not demand that all strangers love you, but only be responsible, fair, and attentive in their dealings with you. Over the centuries, countless attempts have been made to create utopian communities based on generosity and love alone. But in order to survive, all of them were required to define their members' responsibilities to one another through laws and regulations as demanding as those of the world outside.

As confident Christians, you will be responsible and conscientious, and wary of sentimentality that only masquerades as love. If the law is cold, it is at least unsentimental and, therefore, a reliable guide.

Faithfully,

Your father

Chapter 8

Be Compassionate

To the Ancients, Friendship seemed the happiest
and most fully human of all loves;
the crown of life and the school of virtue.
The modern world, in comparison, ignores it.

—C. S. Lewis

Dear Christina, Lisa, and Virginia,

Although law underlies civilized living, you need not consult the statute books prior to every move you make. Even before there was law, there was conscience, and it is your everyday guide to the good life.

Most of what you do every day is morally indifferent, in any case. There is no particular ethical dimension, for example, to sitting down to breakfast, collecting the mail, or writing a letter. Even in moral situations, we do not follow our consciences instinctively, but only consult them for guidance.

When Jesus appealed to his fellow Jews to turn their lives around—to repent and reform—he relied on their knowledge of the law. But when he made a similar appeal to the Gentiles, he counted on their consciences to light their path to goodness. Living as he did in a tiny defeated nation occupied by a pagan army, Jesus often appealed to the conscientious kindness of strangers.

Today, two thousand years later, no one in the Western world can escape having a conscience informed by Christianity. People may deny faith in Jesus, and they may abandon his church, but no one can escape Christian standards of good intent and minimal good behavior. Our laws, our sense of decency, and our everyday relations with our fellow human beings reflect a moral sensibility and a standard that is the legacy of our Christian faith. Secular humanism did not invent compassion, forgiveness, and equal opportunity; Christianity did.

When Jesus appealed to the pagan conscience of his own time, he had less to work with than we do, of course, but still a great deal. The Greeks and Romans were civilized, and they believed in civic and personal virtue. Although the Romans were often cruel, vain, vengeful, and pleasure loving, they revered law, order, loyalty, fortitude, and personal responsibility, and they delighted in beauty, culture, and family life. Pagans praised virtue and prized character. The best of them lived conscientious lives, which is to say they had working consciences. They were reverent, even in the absence of the true God.

As you know, the neighborhood in which you grew up is family oriented. Our neighbors' minivans display bumper stickers that proclaim, "My child is an honor student." But you know, I have yet to see a bumper sticker that says, "My child is a good Christian." That would be presumptuous of both parent and child. What we expect of our children are the same virtues that Roman and Greek parents demanded of their children: dependability, honesty, and fairness among them. Quite apart from imparting faith and hope to our children, we want them to have consciences that will guide them through life.

The Impulse to Goodness

Christianity did not invent good behavior; rather, it builds on our better instincts. The impulse to goodness is in everyone. Civilized life in America is promoted by the law and protected by the courts, the police, and the prisons. But even political leaders consistently urge people to act on idealism, not only on the law. In France, there is even a "Good Samaritan" law that requires passers-by to assist at the scene of an accident. Whatever their religious faith (or doubt), we rely on the kindness of the strangers we meet throughout our lives.

Which is better: a conscience that serves only as an imperfect compass, or a law so stringent that one cannot possibly follow it perfectly? In Jesus' time, the pagans had only their consciences, and the Jews possessed God's law. Neither served them perfectly.

But each operated as a moral compass. Although people routinely fail the dictates of both law and conscience, most of us reluctantly admit our faults, pick ourselves up, and begin again to live true to ourselves, to our loved ones, and to our communities. Confident Christians are further strengthened by a wisdom that neither the Jews nor the pagans possessed: that no failing of ours is so great that it cannot be forgiven by the God who loves us.

It is not religion, however, that demands good behavior of us; rather it is our parents, our neighbors, our employers, and our community. Basic good behavior is nothing more or less than civility, driven by habit and aided by conscience. Bad behavior is punished by the censure of those we love and on whom we depend, and by the state that insists on the responsibility of its members. Religious faith, far from placing an additional moral burden on confident Christians, lightens the weight of mere civil compliance by adding love and forgiveness—the "freedom of the children of God."

God Is the Moral Model

Because Jesus was, among other things, a great moral teacher, many people are inclined to look upon

Christianity as a guide to good behavior. In fact, Christianity subordinates human behavior to God's behavior toward us. The focus of faith is God's graciousness, not human righteousness. Jesus could not have been clearer when he stated that only God is good. The Old Testament testifies to God's faithfulness and his people's infidelity, but the good news of the New Testament is that God so loved the world that he gave his Son to take on our humanity, to walk in our shoes, and to save us from ourselves. Thankful Christians seek to imitate Christ for the sole motive of loving gratitude, not because good behavior will merit a reward.

Jesus' parables and his own behavior testify to God's love for sinners rather than the self-righteous. The Good Shepherd leaves his obedient flock to find the one stray lamb. The Prodigal Son's father celebrates his son's homecoming and forgives him everything. Clearly, goodness consists of responding to God's generosity, not just going through the motions of compliance.

In this respect, Christianity's contrast with Judaism and Islam could not be more striking. In those faiths, men and women act dutifully toward a demanding God, and their God rewards them. Whereas, from Christianity's perspective, God acts in love and forgiveness, and the conscientious Christian responds *in kind.* Granted, only God is good; yet, Jesus calls us to "be perfect, as your heavenly Father is perfect" (Matthew 5:48)—an invitation that makes sense only if we are already conceived in God's image and destined to join him eternally in his perfection.

Of Cats and Children

The great irony is that creatures capable of perversity are nevertheless called to perfection. By contrast, our fellow creatures are innocent and possess only modest aspirations. Admittedly, some animals are fierce, but even the killer shark cannot be accused of cruelty. The behavior of the beasts flows from their design and is intended for their self-preservation. They typically prey on other species, and then only from fear and hunger. Lamentably, we humans are the only creatures capable of being truly beastly, since we alone hate and murder, focusing our savagery on our own kind.

Now that you are adults, having long since left our family nest, your mother and I are left with only four-legged furry "children"—twin kittens and a pedigreed Scottish terrier. Our pets daily present us with object lessons in the differences between people and animals.

Cats are by nature, complacent, private, and dismissive of their fellow creatures. The kittens will soon hunt birds, frogs, and rodents by night, just as our old cats did. It won't be long before your mother and I rise with the sun to discover Fred and Ginger's gifts of dismembered corpses, which they will proudly display on our bedroom carpet, seeking our praise for being so successfully feline. By contrast, Fiona, our Scottish terrier, possesses a dog's special gift for human companionship. Nevertheless, she, like the kittens, marches to a different drummer than you do. Each pet is a creature of instinct. In varying measures, each is disciplined and reliable, but none has the slightest interest in becoming a moral creature.

But to be human is to be capable of moral choices—to act not from design, but from conscience and reflection. For us, choice is inescapable. Whether or not the pets actually ponder in some primitive manner, one thing is certain: they never have *second* thoughts. They never stop to reflect whether they have done the right thing. Your mother and I are inclined to believe that they are affectionate with us, but that may only be our sentimentality showing. In any case, Fiona, Fred, and Ginger do not care for us precisely the way we do for them, because they lack consciences.

Unlike the kittens, Fiona's instinct to please us has produced in her an artificial sense of shame. If our terrier has an accident in the house that requires human clean-up, for example, she will hide in a dark corner, sensing our displeasure. She chooses to punish herself in this modest way lest we consider something more drastic. That is clever of her, but it is only animal intelligence at work.

Some animals are more mature than others, of course, but only in the sense that they take an instinctive responsibility for their offspring and are warier of potential threats. Our neutered pets, for example, who have no offspring to protect and who live in a benign environment, remain blissfully immature, almost childish.

The Childishness of Criminals

Strictly speaking, only *human* children can be accused of being childish. Lacking the beasts' instinct for survival, and dependent on parents for their physical and emotional needs, infants, toddlers, and preschoolers are hapless animals. You once were equally dependent, as were your mother and I before you. Traditionally, Christianity estimates that children must reach the age of seven or eight before they can be expected to make moral choices, for that is the age of reason. Until then, children are largely indulged in their selfishness on the grounds that they do not really know better and are incapable of assessing the impact of their behavior on others.

A very young child's selfishness is not like that of the beasts, being self-indulgent and willful. The nation's prisons are filled with grown-up "children" who never learned to consider the rights and needs of others. Criminals are childish in the sense that they believe that they alone have a right to the good life and are willing to deprive others for the purpose of satisfying themselves. Instead of creating their own satisfaction, they steal it from others. Of course, many noncriminals live self-indulgent lives and manage to stay out of trouble; still, they are unreliable. In time of need, one does not expect kindness from such strangers—and they make fickle friends.

Although animals are sometimes tricked by the unfamiliar, they instinctively know what is good for them. Their selfishness makes sense because it serves its purpose. But self-indulgent men and women are often their own worst enemies, destroying themselves with drugs, alcohol, gluttony, thrill-seeking, and promiscuity.

You do not need to be a Christian to grasp that your first moral responsibility is to yourself. Your responsibility to yourself is not self-indulgence, but only self-preservation and self-respect. But we Christians have an even better motive for taking care of ourselves. Because we realize that we are God's own creatures, made in his image, we assume responsibility for what belongs to God: ourselves.

Everyday Behavior

As Christians, we do not live our lives according to a different set of rules from everyone else. We only act for an additional motive—love. Conscience is common to every human being; we are all guided by rules imprinted in our natures. Conscience impels us—but does not compel us—to be good. We are free to take a different tack, even when it is neither in our interest nor in the interest of anyone else. Christians call such a deviation *sin*, because we have offended God as well as other human beings; others may call it a fault or simply an error. But, inasmuch as we freely chose to go against conscience, it is *our* fault, and it merits some sort of punishment.

Of course, God and the state are not the only instruments of punishment. People punish one another daily, often justifiably, because we have expectations of one another, and failure is irresponsible. You can be fired from your job, for example, or evicted from your apartment.

Sometimes we only complain about unjust treatment, as we do for shoddy service or workmanship. You will send a faulty product back and demand a refund, for example, or I may refuse to tip a surly waiter. When friends are faithless, we often punish them with silence or distance. Unfortunately, people don't come equipped with warranties. We cannot get a refund or a replacement for a friend who has failed us.

Your moral call upon your neighbors does not require that they risk their provenance to save you from debt, but you must trust them to return your lawnmower or ladder or automobile in good order when they borrow it. Everyday morality is often as simple as that. We do not expect saintliness of others, but mere courtesy and trustworthiness. Christians are no more demanding than anyone else in this regard. We may be quicker to forgive but, like everyone else, we are wise not to forget. No one invites repeated trouble.

Good Samaritans

You became Christians as infants by baptism of water and the Holy Spirit. But some Christians experience being "born again" into new life during their teen or adult years. Dramatic as their transformation appears, however, it is not total. None of us goes from sinner to saint overnight, and salvation in any case is not merited, but is a simple gift. We do not need to be baptized to possess a conscience. Baptism only gives us new confidence that we are accepted and forgiven despite our persistent flaws, and provides a powerful new motive to reform our lives through loving service of God and others.

Although humility is the most realistic of virtues, it is not exclusive to Christians. Honest believers can point to unbelievers whose lives are more "Christian" than their own, in the sense of being more generous, compassionate, self-sacrificing, and persistent in service. The kindness of strangers that stems from conscience must not be discounted. We rely on good intentions in ourselves as well, and pray that we have the grace to act on them. It is revealing that the Good Samaritan, that hero of Jesus' parable, was not a Christian. The contemporary world is blessed with many such Good Samaritans.

To be sure, the problem many contemporary Christians have with secular Samaritans is with their choice of victims to aid and the best ways to assist them. The original Samaritan of Jesus' parable happened upon a man beaten and robbed in the road, and saw that the victim was housed and restored to health (see Luke 10:33). Simple enough, and commendable. But what of today's AIDS victims and pregnant teenagers? What about the teeming and hungry populations of the Third World? Secular Samaritans often prescribe condoms, abortion, and mercy killing, whereas many Christians believe such quick compassion poorly serves the victims and only encourages the underlying evils that prompted the problems in the first place.

If so, then Christian Good Samaritans must come up with better solutions. Here as elsewhere, conscience is not a foolproof guide, nor are the churches always in agreement. Happily, however, secular and Christian humanists tend to focus on the same victims and our obligation to serve them. They only disagree at times on how to do it effectively. Indifference to those in need would be the greater evil.

The Virtues of Friends and Strangers

Few of us, Christian or otherwise, impose the highest moral standards when we choose our friends, which is just as well; otherwise we would have few close companions. We know our friends' faults, and can be sure that they know ours. We routinely ignore those flaws or forgive them, however, as friends will, because such imperfections are beside the point.

Friendships persist even as marriages break down, because friends, unlike lovers, are neither exclusive nor possessive of one another. Friends have common interests and find one another interesting—ingredients sometimes missing in a marriage. Beyond that, friendship demands only mutual candor, fidelity, and a modicum of generosity and availability—secular virtues, to be sure—but surprisingly rare in contemporary society. Friends are comfortable with each other.

There are few greater blessings in this life than the gift of companionship, but you needn't idealize friendship. (There is even honor among thieves, after all, and criminals choose other malefactors for friends!) In any case, you cannot aspire to be a friend to everyone in the world, but you can be a kindly and compassionate stranger. Pope John Paul II and Mother Teresa were friends because they shared so many interests and beliefs; moreover, they enjoyed each other's company. They did not minister to each other's needs, however, but both helped others.

During my unsuccessful sojourn in the ministry, I made the mistake of believing that I had to be the friend of everyone who sought my help professionally. Adding that false dimension to service only hampered my ability to help them and their ability to accept my counsel and help. Only politicians pretend to be friends to everyone. You can show Christian love to needy strangers without befriending them, or even liking them.

When a stranger has stopped to help me with a flat tire or when one of your teachers went out of her way to help you with a lesson, I did not jump to the conclusion that this Samaritan was being "Christian." People's motives are often unfathomable. More often than not, you and I act well or badly from habit, not from some sudden gush of philanthropy or malevolence. When some parents objected to the long-standing requirement of the Boy Scouts of America that all members profess belief in God, they were not attempting to infest that venerable institution with amoral boys. Rather, they were only insisting on a point that we all acknowledge: that goodness (and its opposite) have their roots in conscience, not in religion.

You were all Girl Scouts yourselves. When a Scout does you a good deed, you do not inquire about her theology or her churchgoing habits. You simply thank her and reflect that two thousand years of Christianity has educated the human conscience. We are better off for our faith (whether or not we practice it) precisely because faith has inclined us to be faithful to one another.

Scout's Honor

When I was a boy, I joined the Scouts and took the pledge to be on "Scout's honor" throughout my life. It didn't seem onerous at the time, but just the decent thing to do. The very notion of belonging to a group implies a duty to one's fellows and to the community. Duty runs deep. Growing up as an only child, with no brothers or sisters to compete with, I found it remarkable that my friends, who routinely fought with their siblings, immediately stood up for them when anyone outside their families challenged them.

Although my friends teased their brothers mercilessly, they were quick to fight for their honor. I had to wait to have children of my own to experience how each of you, competing individually for attention, became a team when one of you was threatened. Tribal and familial solidarity are much older than Christianity, and we depend upon them for civilized life.

About the same time I joined the Scouts, I also was introduced to the Christian catechism and was forced to memorize its first precept: "The purpose of life is to know, to love, and to serve God in this world, and to be happy with him in the next." This proposition was harder to swallow than Scout's honor. After all, how could I manage to live my life for someone as remote and invisible as my Creator in hopes of a reward that consists of living eternally with this mysterious, demanding being? It was not this child's idea of an entertaining life or a satisfactory eternity.

While keeping this heresy from my teachers, I quietly accepted that the purpose of life was to know, love, and serve *myself*, and to be happy *now*. I reckoned that I could still keep my Scout's honor to serve others in need, yet be good to myself first of all. God seemed to be beside the point. He could take care of himself; he didn't need me.

What I didn't realize then is that the solitary pursuit of happiness is doomed from the outset. Adulthood taught me that—as I suspect it is teaching you. There are plenty of pleasures this side of the grave, many of them quite innocent, but they will elude your determined pursuit of them. C. S. Lewis compared happiness to the bubbles in a glass of champagne, which can't be grasped or saved, only enjoyed and lost. That is not the fault of the champagne, and it is no solution to keep the bottle corked and hoard the bubbles. Present satisfaction is real, but fleeting; and its source and culmination must be elsewhere. So I returned to the catechism as an adult to see how I had reckoned wrongly.

If God wants me to know, love, and serve him in this world, I finally decided, it must be possible to do so, and my effort must be for my benefit, not his. He doesn't need me; so I must need him. If my Creator himself is to be my reward, then he, better than anyone else, knows what will really satisfy me.

But why must we wait for the big payoff? Because we are not ready. Just as we cannot approach calculus without first mastering arithmetic and algebra, we cannot grasp God and his happiness until we are virtuous. And virtue is something more than Scout's honor. Good behavior builds character only when we consistently do the right things for the right reasons. God, C. S. Lewis assures us, does not demand obedience to a set of rules; rather, he is interested in a particular sort of *person*—one who not only does kind things generously, but whose nature is kind. That sort of person will never be a stranger to his Creator nor to his fellow creatures. That is the sort of person you aspire to be.

Forgiveness

The Golden Rule does not belong to Christianity, nor to any religion. To treat others as we would have them treat us is sound morality, and it is ingrained in our consciences even when we take the occasional vacation from our better judgment and treat others badly or with indifference.

But the Golden Rule is by no means the last word in morality, because it lacks two ingredients that confident Christians must add to it: forgiveness and love. It is one thing for you to deal with others as you would have them deal with you; but what if a person has already treated you badly and has become your "enemy"? The Old Testament offered an answer. It allowed a fair measure of revenge: not death for a mere slight, but eye for eye, tooth for tooth. But the New Testament demands more than fairness; it insists that we forgive—and even love—our enemies.

How is this possible? For starters, Christians are advised to hate the sin but love the sinner. That is no simple task when we are the ones who have been sinned against. Yet, we have plenty of practice in making this distinction, because it is precisely how we treat ourselves! Moral persons do not make excuses for themselves but, rather, acknowledge their faults with regret, then forgive themselves and get back to living, trying to do better next time. If you did not forgive yourself, you would soon become your own worst enemy and be incapable of resuming your life. It is imperative that we forgive ourselves; otherwise we would be crippled with guilt.

Likewise it is imperative that we forgive our enemies. We pray, "Forgive us our sins as we forgive those who sin against us," confident that, by forgiving our enemies, we will receive God's forgiveness. What makes pardoning so onerous is that, in real life, our enemies have no notion that they require our forgiveness and, in any case, are unlikely to forgive us in return. You've been in this situation many times, asking yourself, "How can I forgive someone who has no sense of shame or guilt?" What's more: "How can I bring myself to love that person?"

The only way is to borrow God's perspective. God is perfectly aware of our faults, as well as those of our enemies, but he loves us all and forgives us all. God is the Great Leveler of the moral playing field. Christians must play the game his way, which is the way of forgiveness and love. We are now far beyond the morality that relies on mere conscience and the kindness of strangers. We are on the cross with Jesus, who forgave his executioners because "they do not know what they are doing."

Mohandas Gandhi understood the limitations of the old morality. If those who are threatened and victimized continue to demand an eye for an eye, he predicted, "the world would be blind." There is a surer way to live than by law and conscience alone, and Jesus reveals it in his Sermon on the Mount. The subject of my next letter will be love. Until then, know that I love you.

Faithfully,

Your father

Chapter 9

Seek Perfection

Will it alter my life altogether?
O tell me the truth about love.

—W. H. Auden

Dear Christina, Lisa, and Virginia,

I was especially sad when I read of the death of Leo Buscaglia, at the age of seventy-four. By all accounts, this man's passing from life was peaceful, and he was prepared. He once proclaimed that death "is only morbid if you never lived." That was not his problem, because he lived his life to the brim. If you recall him from his television appearances, he looked a little like Winnie the Pooh (with a beard), and was popularly known as "Dr. Hug," because he literally embraced everyone with whom he came into contact.

Buscaglia started out as a special education teacher in California. I wish you could have been his students when you were struggling to overcome your own handicaps in the classroom. Later, when he taught at the University of Southern California, Buscaglia created a course called "Love 101." It wasn't about sex, but about caring and sharing. He believed that love was the single unifying force in life, and wrote more than a dozen books about the subject—books that have been translated into twenty languages.

The truth about love is that it will change your life altogether if you let it. Love is sometimes passionate, occasionally sentimental, but always ardent and true. It is the subject of nearly every song and poem, as well as many stories. Lamentably, love has many imposters, but over time I trust you will unmask them. Love is not the prisoner of romance, but a loving person can make all of her life a romance. Although everyone wants love, it is not for sale. You have to produce it yourself, then give it freely. In this, as in so many other things, Jesus set the standard for you.

"How they love one another!" people remarked of the early Christians, and it is clear that they did. It was equally clear *why* they made love the rule of their lives: because God so loved the world that he gave his only Son to it. The only proper response to love is love.

Today, alas, it is not so obvious that Christians love one another, or that we love others beyond our faith. Love is risky; accordingly, we mete out our affections, weighing the risks that our caring will be wasted and unrequited. Anyone coming across the story of Jesus for the first time could easily make the case that he made a fool of himself for love. He was love's victim, literally killed for caring. If he hadn't loved so much, he wouldn't have died. But as Christians, we realize that love triumphs even over death. Jesus proved it. You will want to prove it as well in your own lives.

The Sermon on the Mount

Jesus' gospel of love is exemplified in his Sermon on the Mount. Isn't it odd that Jesus' sermon is admired as sublime moral teaching by Christians and non-Christians alike the world over, but universally ignored? As a young child, I was taught to regard the sermon's Beatitudes as only "counsels of perfection"—guidelines applicable to saints but too strenuous for ordinary believers like me, who have trouble enough following the Ten Commandments. The consequence is that Jesus' example is treated with honor and benign neglect, an irony that prompted G. K. Chesterton to affirm that Christianity has not been tried and found wanting; it has been found difficult and left untried.

Does Jesus seriously expect you to be poor, humble, and merciful, as well as pure, long-suffering, and pacific—or are these options, like automobile accessories, to be purchased at extra cost? Must you not only forgive your enemies, but love them as well? Must you deny not only your bodies, but your minds, expunging lust and hatred altogether from your hearts? In short, can you make love the rule of your lives?

That nuns and monks take vows of poverty, chastity, and obedience appears to argue that only unattached, unworldly, and idealistic men and women can effectively aspire to Jesus' lifestyle of love. But in expounding the Beatitudes, Jesus was uncharacteristically clear and uncompromising. Elsewhere in the Gospels he often shrouded his moral teaching in metaphor. By contrast, in the Sermon on the Mount, Jesus suddenly spoke clearly. These are not suggestions; they are prescriptions.

Consider the scene of the sermon. Jesus, surrounded by his disciples, addressed the multitudes. The synopsis alone of his sermon extends through three complete chapters (5, 6 and 7) of Matthew's Gospel, so there is nothing offhanded about it. Throughout, Jesus neither harangued his listeners nor patronized them. Nor did he give them orders. He did not tell them what to *do*, but how things *are*. He did not say, "Impoverish yourselves!" but rather proclaimed that "the poor are blessed."

Traditional translations miss the full force of Jesus' language, which is that the poor are not just blessed, but are "lucky," "fortunate," "happy." To be sure, Jesus is not saying that by embracing poverty, people will achieve happiness, but rather that the poor are *already* happy. How can that be? How can anyone be deemed fortunate to be in misfortune? How can victims be victors over their circumstances?

The answer is that those who seek first the kingdom of heaven will have their fill. There is no virtue in being deprived; but, having nothing of their own, the poor look wholly to God for their fill. He alone is their reward. The same goes for all the other privations that Jesus called "blessed." Just as there are no atheists in foxholes, there is no alternative to God in desperate circumstance. We are blessed in our emptiness because nothing but God can fill it.

Admittedly, for most people most of the time, God is the object of last resort, to be consulted in trouble. But for those Jesus mentioned in his sermon, God is their first and *only* resort. This is precisely what Jesus himself acknowledged when, dying on the cross, he proclaimed to his Father: "Into your hands I commend my spirit" (Luke 23:46).

The Destiny of the Faithful

The Sermon on the Mount tells you less about yourselves than it tells you about God. You are to be perfect because God is perfect. You are to forgive because God forgives. You are to love because God first loved you. You are to live free from anxiety because God sustains you. You are to "store up for yourselves treasures in heaven" rather than "treasures on earth" because "where your treasure is, there your heart will be also" (Matthew 6:19–21).You are to pray ceaselessly, because God never sleeps, but stands ever ready to answer your prayers.

It is tempting to pretend to stand squarely on your own two feet, but you run the risk of forgetting that God gave you those feet. It is tempting to be self-satisfied, whereas only God can offer assurance. It is tempting to act independently, although independence is the big lie that has afflicted humankind since Eden. It is tempting to simply play by the rules and count on a final payoff, tit-for-tat, without acknowledging that love is the only rule that covers every situation in life.

The Sermon on the Mount identifies the lie in these temptations by underscoring your utter reliance on God. You are blessed when you grasp how dependent you are on the only dependable being in the universe.

As a young child, I was taught that my prayers of petition were signs of weakness and presumption. I was told that loving God, thanking God, and seeking God's forgiveness were the only worthy motives for prayer, and that begging was unseemly and selfish. But in his sermon, Jesus said that Christians must pray even for their daily bread! A local televangelist is fond of urging his flock to pray only for big things and not bother God for small favors. He misses the point—that God is the source of all our needs and favors. It will not do to pretend that you rely on God for only the big things; you depend on him for *everything*.

Christina, you've worked with the homeless and you live a spartan life paying off your loans for graduate school. All three of you struggle on small incomes. But you know that poverty is more than a measure of how much money people have in their bank accounts. Poverty comes in many forms—emotional, physical, spiritual—and in one way or another we are all impoverished.

Properly understood, faith transforms poverty into opportunity for deeper communion with God. In our direst moments, especially those that are flung upon us, we come face to face with our limitations and recognize our complete dependence upon God. And in these moments we unite with God, who draws us beyond ourselves to become more than we are at present.

Of course, we do not recognize our dependence on God only in extremities. There are those who *willingly* empty themselves, such as choosing financial poverty for example, to make room for God. And they are blessed by the fact of their poverty only because they have voluntarily emptied their lives to make room for God.

When we empty ourselves to make room for God, we become like God. We pour out our being as God poured out the divine Being in Christ. No trace of selfishness remains. To use the words of John Macquarrie in his *Principles of Christian Theology*, heaven "is the reward of having been delivered from any seeking for rewards." The only reward for self-giving love is an increased capacity for it.

The Disciples

If, as I was taught, the Beatitudes prescribe an impossible way of life for the ordinary Christian, how can we account for the multitudes who flocked to Jesus to listen to him, sometimes for days at a time? It surely was not in hopes of a magic show. Jesus was sparing with his miracles and never used them to add spice to his preaching. His teaching stood on its own.

No, the multitudes remained rapt because they recognized that some among them were already poor, humble, and persecuted like their Master. These few were the disciples, who had literally dropped everything to heed Jesus' invitation to follow him. Recall the rich man who, acknowledging that he already obeyed the law, asked Jesus what else he must do to secure eternal life. Jesus replied:

> *If you want to be perfect, go now and sell your property and give the money away to the poor—you will have riches in heaven. Then come and follow me!* (Matthew 19:21)

When the man walked away "crestfallen" because he could not contemplate parting with his wealth, Jesus made his celebrated remark about the difficulties the rich would encounter entering heaven, but concluded:

> *Humanly speaking, it is impossible; but with God anything is possible* (vs. 25–26).

This, however, did not satisfy the apostle Peter. "Look," he said, "we have left everything and followed you. What is that going to be worth to us?" (v. 27). Jesus reassured his disciples that those who impoverish themselves for his sake will receive everything in return many times over, and inherit eternal life.

So, will only the poor be rewarded? No: "With God everything is possible." But those who call out to God from their poverty will surely be filled. Even now, they will be filled with love.

The multitudes on the mountain grasped that these few unprepossessing men were the persons Jesus was talking about, because they had nothing but him. The disciples were already living the Sermon on the Mount.

The Apostles

Nothing about Jesus' recruits suggests that they possessed the strength of character sufficient, even with grace, to live the Sermon on the Mount. What could Jesus have seen in the twelve apostles? We know that the largest contingent consisted of fishermen, and one was a tax collector. Legend suggests that the others included a carpenter, a plasterer, a druggist, and a tanner. One of the Twelve, Judas Iscariot, whatever his former profession, was entrusted with the group's paltry finances.

For the most part, this tiny band was uneducated and slow-witted; yet each apostle was handpicked by the most sophisticated person who ever lived. What bound them all was their unhesitating willingness to suspend their personal and professional lives to follow Jesus. The vanity, thickheadedness, petty ambition, jealousy, and inconstancy that marked their daily life with Jesus are echoed today in the lives of ordinary Christians like ourselves who make the *decision* to follow Christ but are not thereby instantly transformed into saints.

In part, it is the self-deprecating portraits of the apostles that make the gospel accounts so credible. If men so flawed as these could make such a total commitment of themselves to Jesus, it speaks volumes about the character of the Person to whom they pledged their lives. If such ordinary persons were chosen by Jesus for lives of perfection, then the Sermon on the Mount applies to all Christians and qualifies as the ultimate source of your confidence and mine.

The sermon speaks first of all to these men who, day in and day out, exemplified the poverty, meekness, forgiveness, love, and peacemaking that Jesus pronounced blessed. Remember that Jesus did not point to his companions' personal virtue, but to the conditions in which they lived and the perilous mission they had undertaken. As his followers, they could not *help* but be poor and persecuted, and they could not escape his example.

These were the same men who jockeyed for Jesus' favor, who dozed while their Master prayed to escape death, who fled when he was arrested, who denied they even knew him, and who initially doubted his Resurrection. Yet, despite their inconstancy, they defined their lives by him alone and so lived out the sermon, because they put their entire faith in him.

Incidentally, as women, don't read anything into the fact that these Twelve were all men. At the time, men were freer to travel with Jesus and to sleep in the open fields. If anything, the women in the Gospels tend to come off better than the men. The rule of love knows no gender.

Embracing Poverty

Cuban dictator Fidel Castro once remarked that Karl Marx, the prophet of Communism, "would have agreed with the Sermon on the Mount." He was wrong. Communism is based on the forcible *abolition* of poverty, not on its voluntary acceptance. It is an ideology that seeks to make men and women gods, controlling their own destiny, independent of their Creator. While purporting to be motivated by compassion, Communism resorted to terror from the outset. In a parody of Christian love, it enforced mere comradeship. Robbing from the rich to give to the poor, Communism managed to leave almost everyone impoverished. Far from suffering persecution for justice's sake, it created the terrible Gulag.

What Marx did believe was that religion is the "opiate of the people," drugging the masses into accepting their present miseries for the sake of future reward. Let's acknowledge that he had a point, notably in the Victorian society in which Marx lived and wrote. Victorians managed at once to be callous and sentimental about poverty. The poor, they liked to believe, were childlike; with industry, they could better themselves. But if they remained in need, it was either their own choice or God's judgment on them. Lamentably, the Church did little at the time to disenchant the rich about their prejudices.

Marx's contemporary, George Bernard Shaw (like Dickens before him), objected to this hypocrisy. Poverty, he said, is "the greatest of evils and the worst of crimes . . . I can't take religion to a man with bodily hunger in his eyes."

Setting aside its Victorian aberration, the Church takes a sensible rather than a sentimental view of poverty. It preaches that the poor are unfortunate through no fault of their own and must be ministered to. Poverty is like a mutating virus: it assumes many forms, so that even when physical hunger is abated and health is restored, the human spirit may remain starved. Although it deplores human want, the Church also senses that poverty, *freely embraced*, can enrich the human spirit: "If anyone wants to follow in my footsteps he must give up all rights to himself, take up his cross and follow me" (Matthew 16:24).

In your quest for confidence, you need not construct crosses of your own; your lives will be littered with troubles not of your making but which you cannot ignore. If you spend your time trying to grind your crosses into sawdust, you will be thwarted. Jesus suggests that the better course is to pick them up and follow him. That is the way of love.

The Value of Simplicity

Saint Francis of Assisi, whose genius consisted of finding treasure in the commonplace, is perhaps the most respected exponent of voluntary poverty. Nevertheless, everyone who has embraced a simpler life has made the same point—that our wealth consists of appreciation, not possession. The poverty that Jesus exalts in the Sermon on the Mount is not grinding need, but radical simplicity. Saint Francis treated his condition chivalrously, addressing his simplicity as a loving companion: his "Lady Poverty." He treated life as a romance.

Even those who disdain the simple life understand the saint's value of appreciation over mere possession. Connoisseurs sip their wine slowly, and gourmets savor their food in small portions. True lovers do not rape; rather, they revere their beloved. Just so, you will simplify your lives the better to appreciate your blessings, and lighten the burden of your possessions so you will have more strength to bear your inevitable crosses. By clearing your vision of clutter, you will see the path your Master takes, and cleanse your hearts to make room for God's love. By means of such practical alchemy, poverty will become pure gold.

Alarmed that World War II was ended with the horrible sacrifice of the civilians of Hiroshima and Nagasaki, Omar Bradley, the chairman of the joint chiefs of staff, lamented, "We have grasped the mystery of the atom and rejected the Sermon on the Mount." To accept the sermon, confident Christians must reject "all rights to themselves" in favor of God's rights to their lives, in certain hope that God will be their reward.

Unfortunately, models of poverty such as St. Francis and Mother Teresa are difficult to emulate. They founded religious brotherhoods and sisterhoods of celibates pledged to a common life and mutual support. The typical Christian who seeks to live confidently is more likely to be a married man or woman with family responsibilities, bills to pay, and an employer who seeks something other than the kingdom of heaven. In his personal search for the meaning of the Sermon on the Mount, Philip Yancey fixed on the example set by two laymen, the celebrated Russian novelists Leo Tolstoy and Fyodor Dostoevsky, each of whom attempted to live the sermon. Tolstoy's *War and Peace* and Dostoevsky's *The Brothers Karamazov* are arguably the greatest novels ever written.

The Two Russian Disciples

While Tolstoy ultimately failed in his attempt to live the sermon literally, he never lost faith in Jesus' call to follow him. It was his literalness that betrayed the writer in his quest. He conceived of the sermon as a set of rules for perfection, and created even more stringent rules for himself in an effort to be disciplined. Acknowledging that he was a rich man, he freed his indentured servants, abandoned royalties from his books, and gave away the bulk of his great estate. He dressed like a poor man, made his own shoes and clothing, and tilled the fields for food with his own hands.

In his single-minded quest for perfection, Tolstoy inexplicably ignored the people closest to him, virtually impoverishing his family. Without consulting his wife, he made public vows of chastity and sought to sleep separate from her. His repeated failure was apparent, inasmuch as she endured sixteen pregnancies. She complained that "there is so little genuine warmth in him; his kindness does not come from the heart, but merely from his principles." The great novelist treated love like the law.

But it is premature to convict Tolstoy of hypocrisy, for he was the first to admit his moral failures. Indeed, he not only intended good, but accomplished a great deal of it, albeit more in the service of humanity than of the individuals who depended on him. He kept faith in his ideals, even when he failed repeatedly to honor them. Late in life, lamenting his weaknesses, he hid all the ropes and guns on his estate lest he succumb to despair and attempt to kill himself. In the end, according to Philip Yancey in his book *The Jesus I Never Knew,* Tolstoy fled family and fortune to die a ragged vagrant, still condemning himself and defending Jesus' sermon. In later life he wrote a friend:

> *Look at my present life and then at my former life, and you will see that I do attempt to carry out (Christ's precepts). It is true that I have not fulfilled one thousandth part of them, and I am ashamed of this, but I have failed to fulfill them not because I did not wish to, but because I was unable to . . . Attack me, I do this myself, but attack me rather than the path I follow . . .*

Tolstoy's error lay in following the sermon as an exercise in self-improvement—a do-it-yourself project destined to fail because it can't be done alone.

Long before the Russian's odyssey, the apostle Paul had attempted a life of perfection only to discover his inner conflict between aspiration and action. To the apostle's credit, Paul grasped that the gap could be bridged only by grace. Perfection cannot be pursued and won; rather, we can only open our lives to the gift of grace and be drawn to God on God's own initiative. The sermon demonstrates how to trust God's grace to cover our inadequacies.

Tolstoy, like the Jews, trusted in his own ability to adhere to law to win salvation, rather than accept Redemption as God's gift of grace and love.

As a young man, Fyodor Dostoevsky was less admirable than Tolstoy, but in later life no one better understood the grace of forgiveness and love. As a young prodigal, Dostoevsky drank and gambled to excess, harming his health and depleting his fortune. Plotting revolution, he was arrested by the tsar and sentenced to death. At the last instant, as he stood blindfolded and tied to a post before a firing squad, his sentence was commuted to hard labor.

It was a moment of grace few of us experience in life. Reconciled to imminent death, he received back his life as a gift, and he promised himself: "Now my life will change; I shall be born again in a new form." As a convict in Siberia for ten years, the young revolutionary was allowed only one book, the New Testament, and its pages persuaded him that God gives us all a second chance.

Dostoevsky's inclination to believe in man's essential innocence was sorely tested by prison life in the company of vicious criminals. Yet, he learned to glimpse God in the worst of them and became convinced that "We love him because he first loved us" (1 John 4:19). In *The Brothers Karamazov* he affirmed, "I do not know the answer to the problem of evil, but I do know love."

From Tolstoy, Philip Yancey grasped the need to look to the Kingdom of God within himself. From Dostoevsky, he learned that not only the Kingdom of God can be found there, but that Christ himself dwells within us. The only way to resolve the tension between the Sermon on the Mount and flawed human nature is to accept that you will never measure up—and that you do not have to, because grace will be sufficient. The account has already been paid in advance for you by Christ.

The Seduction of Easy Grace

Still, that is no excuse for complacency. There is such a thing as cheap grace, and it is too often mistaken for the real thing. Cheap grace is born of indifference, not confidence. It is Christianity taken for granted, not living in Christ. The twentieth-century martyr, Dietrich Bonhoeffer, identified it as grace without a price tag. To be sure, the Sermon on the Mount reassures us that God gives his grace freely, but experience demonstrates that we accept it only with difficulty. Grace, although free, is costly because it requires us, in Jesus' words, to "put on my yoke and learn from me" (Matthew 11:29). But in the next breath, Jesus reassured us that his yoke is sweet and his burden is light.

Bonhoeffer experienced firsthand the poverty and persecution that Jesus blessed in his sermon. Arrested in 1943 for opposing the Nazis, the German pastor ministered to his fellow prisoners in a series of concentration camps and was executed in Flosenburg on April 9, 1945, only a few days before the camp's liberation by the Allies. Because he lived and died bearing Jesus' yoke, Bonhoeffer was quick to sense the easy heresies that falsify the Sermon on the Mount.

Merely assenting to faith, he insisted, is not being faithful. Believing in Christianity makes no sense unless one is faithful to Jesus himself. Christianity is not an ideology; it is the love of Christ. Cheap grace, Bonhoeffer maintained, pretends that sin can be forgiven without repentance. Cheap grace, he said, does not come from God at all; rather, it is the grace we bestow upon ourselves. Cheap grace is grace without discipleship, grace without discipline, grace without the yoke and the cross, grace without the living, loving Christ.

Whereas the grace that enables us to live the Sermon on the Mount is costly. In Jesus' metaphor, it is the treasure hidden in the field, for the sake of which a man will sell all he owns. It is the pearl of great price for which a merchant will expend his entire fortune. Jesus assures you that if you will but knock, the door will be opened to you. But it remains closed until you announce yourselves, then persist until you gain entry. Rest assured, the kingdom is worth the effort. *Grace is costly because it cost God the life of his Son*. That God did not reckon this a price too great to pay for you and me only underscores the high cost of following Jesus.

Persistence is the key. Jesus called twice on Peter to follow him, first at the outset of Jesus' ministry, then again following his Resurrection. Between the initial and final calls, Peter had proclaimed Jesus' divinity, then denied that he had ever met him. Peter plunged from fidelity to betrayal, yet Jesus renewed his invitation, and the apostle went on to follow his Master so literally that he, too, died on a cross.

Costly Grace

Grace demands discipleship—not instant perfection, but persistence. When our Western world became Christianized, the Church began to act as if it were the sole repository and dispenser of grace, cutting God out of the picture. Ironically, the growth of monasticism, far from attracting Christians to the ideals of the Sermon on the Mount, lulled them into complacency, because it suggested that discipleship was an *option*, suitable for poor monks and nuns, leaving the everyday Christian with worldly concerns, navigating life on the fuel of cheap grace.

Once Christianity became institutionalized, it became tempting to think of religion as a matter of membership, and the Church as a kind of club. One was a Christian by dint of keeping up one's membership and observing the house rules. What was lost was the true definition of Christianity as discipleship. Don't you think it's significant that the word "Christian" was never uttered by Jesus? "It was in Antioch that the disciples were first given the name of 'Christians'" (Acts 11:26). But the word "disciple" occurs repeatedly in Jesus' speech, along with his invitation, "Follow me!" The Sermon on the Mount defines the Christian as the disciple who personally follows Jesus.

Preaching on the mountainside, Jesus startled the multitudes when he referred to his ever-so-ordinary disciples as "blessed." In fact, the lives of these ordinary men had become extraordinary. They had left everything, claiming Jesus as their sole possession, answering his call and clinging to his promise. For that call and that promise, they were prepared to endure anything and everything with Jesus.

Bonhoeffer warns us that it is misleading to find beatitude in the disciples' mere *behavior*. They were not blessed because they were good. Rather, it is Jesus' invitation and his reward that are blessed; and the disciples partook of blessedness because they followed him and hoped in him. Already, they had become strangers in this world because their treasure awaited them elsewhere. For the pearl of great price, they had renounced not only personal possessions but personal rights. They no longer expected peace but persecution for their choice. They no longer sought honor but accepted the world's disdain. Pure in heart, they had reverted to the childlike innocence of Adam and Eve before the Fall. Their hearts were no longer ruled by law or conscience alone, but by the will of Jesus.

To what conclusion can such a life lead? Clearly to the cross, but only as a way station to the kingdom of heaven. The kingdom was the disciples' distant lodestar, yet miraculously they found God's kingdom within themselves. So can you.

Whereas complacent Christians take leave of this world only reluctantly, hoping for consolation in the next, disciples *know* that the best is yet to be and devote their lives joyfully to the kingdom. To his disciples Jesus said, "Be glad, then, yes, be tremendously glad, for your reward in heaven is magnificent" (Matthew 5:12).

Salt of the Earth

That does not make Christianity other-worldly. Although Jesus' disciples sought first the kingdom of heaven, Jesus called them the salt of the *earth* and the light of the *world* (see Matthew 5:13), because their mission was here. They were not guided by a law superior to that followed by the Jews, but by the same law of love with this difference: they could see the law observed perfectly by Jesus.

As he extended his sermon, Jesus not only extolled the old law but expanded it—to all appearances making it even more onerous to be a Christian than to be a Jew. In fact, Jesus was only inviting his followers to change their minds and hearts instead of merely going through the motions of law-abiding. Hatred and lust, he said, can no more be tolerated than murder and adultery. Because guilty people take oaths in their defense to protect their lies, their protestations of innocence must be replaced by honesty: "Whatever you have to say, let your 'yes' be a plain 'yes' and your 'no' be a plain 'no'" (Matthew 5:37).

Revenge, Jesus noted, is unwarranted, even against the most evil provocations. What Gandhi, Martin Luther King, Jr., and Nelson Mandela learned from the sermon is that evil eventually collapses when it is not violently resisted, and one's enemies are ultimately disarmed by love and forgiveness. The disciples, incidentally, had a powerful reason for forgiving their enemies: they themselves had denied and abandoned Jesus, making themselves God's enemies. Yet, in a poignant lesson, God forgave them.

Does this mean that you must be pacifists? In your strictly personal lives, yes—there is no room for hatred or revenge in Jesus' disciple. But you must also be realists like Jesus who, while turning the other cheek, acknowledged the evil of his tormentors. When Jesus violently cast out the money changers from the Temple, he was acting for God and the purity of religion, not simply for himself. It is notable that Jesus took pains neither to condemn soldiering nor the right of people to defend themselves. Jesus' pacifism led inexorably to the cross upon which he was victimized. He did not resist; yet he conquered.

Conflict is a fact of life, and you are God's stewards, responsible for preserving his creation. Just as environmentalists refuse to allow the selfish to spoil the seas, the soil, and the air, you will defend your families, communities, and nation against evil. You will look to heaven for good without abandoning the world to evil. But you will defend those you love in a spirit of reverence, not hatred or revenge. And in your strictly personal lives, you will be moved by love and humility, not by anger and righteousness.

The Way of Wisdom

Over the course of two millennia, the Sermon on the Mount has suffered many interpretations in misguided attempts to soften its strictures. Even a cursory reading of Jesus' words suggests that his instructions are uncompromisingly clear. Far from being a polite guide to Christian etiquette, his sermon is a rigorous design for a life of total dedication and discipleship.

Two questions remain to be answered, however: Is such a life *practicable*? And is it *necessary*, or can a confident Christian get by with something less rigorous?

To the first: Jesus would not call us to perfection if it were not the preferred path to take. The alternative is to embrace our inadequacies. Perfection is elusive this side of eternity, but that does not excuse us from accepting the gift of costly grace that will bind us more closely to our Creator. In any event, the sermon bids you to seek *his* perfection, not your own.

In one important respect, the sermon is an inadequate guide. It gives proper direction and attitude, but it does not tell us how to behave and choose in every moral circumstance. Asking yourself "What would Jesus do?" in daily crises may only make them worse. Instead, in times of uncertainty, emulate the heart and mind of Jesus, admitting humbly that sometimes you will do more harm than good, requiring you to beg the forgiveness of those you have tried to help. Shrinking from moral decisions is seldom a safe alternative; discipleship demands involvement.

Living the Sermon on the Mount is practicable because it seeks your only true objective—the kingdom—and is enabled by grace and forgiveness. Although faltering is inevitable, confident Christians keep their eyes on the prize. The prize is not yours to be *won*, however, but only to be accepted gratefully as a gift.

To the second: of course you can get by with less effort and dedication than Jesus' disciples, but at the expense of diverting your lives from their purpose, drifting without a destination. Humanly speaking, there are many gods to worship in this life, but only one God who can deliver. There is nothing wrong with seeking wealth, success, and pleasure in your lives, but it is misguided to believe that anything good will come your way through your own efforts alone.

Life is neither a game to be won nor a lottery that pays off. All good comes from God's grace, and he is the only Prize worth having. Ask yourselves: What can come at the end of lives that are focused on the transient, when the kingdom is eternal? If you have not sought the kingdom, you will risk not recognizing it when it is offered to you.

Can you and I get by with living less than the Sermon on the Mount? Yes, but that admission only raises a further question: Will complacent Christians who have placed their entire faith in this life be prepared to accept the gift of eternal life when it is offered to them? We can only take Jesus at his word: "Humanly speaking, it is impossible; but with God everything is possible." I urge you to seek God's perfection in your own lives. Let love alter your lives altogether.

Faithfully,

Your father

Part IV

Confidence

Let there be a place somewhere
in which you can breathe naturally, quietly,
and not have to take your breath
in continuous short gasps.
A place where your mind can be idle
and forget its concerns,
descend into silence,
and worship the Father in secret.

—Thomas Merton

Chapter 10

When Your Faith Falters

It isn't that they can't see the solution.
It is that they can't see the problem.

—G. K. Chesterton

Dear Christina, Lisa, and Virginia,

When I began these letters to you, my intention was to strengthen your confidence in the faith you live—and that remains my dearest wish. But you will notice that nowhere have I attempted to prove the truth of your religion; instead, I have sought to increase your appreciation of the operative Christian virtues of faith, hope, and love. Christianity can't be verified in the usual ways; rather, it is founded on faith and "proved" by practice.

Your confidence will grow not from reason or scientific observation, but from viewing your lives from God's point of view. Spiritual writers call it "putting on the mind of Christ." If you are faithful, hopeful, and loving in your lives, you will also be confident. You will be living your religion.

Don't let your confidence falter because friends whom you admire are indifferent to God and believe the practice of religion to be superstitious or even pernicious. The truth of your faith is not a function of intelligence but of fidelity—God's faith in you and your faith in him. You are able to view faith from the *inside*—an advantage missing to Christianity's critics. Others may demand of you, "How can you believe these things?" Your answer will be, "There is nothing better to be believed." And: "To believe nothing is to live without hope."

Your weakest reason for being a Christian is that you have always been one, because that is mindless faith and it cannot survive doubt. Confidence is not complacency, nor is Christianity a hobby or fashion. Rather, your faith explains the way things *are*, which is another way of saying what is true. Confident Christians seek to be true. With confidence you will experience your faith more fully, complete your conversion, and awake each day to live in the light of eternity.

Confidence is not a weapon to wield in the face of the faithless. I have encountered Christian apologists who marshal logic and Scripture in an attempt to vanquish skeptics. Their erudition can be occasionally devastating, but it is ultimately impotent. No one can be beaten into submitting to faith, because faith is a gift—and confidence is not certainty. Faith cannot be imposed, but only accepted. Confident Christians exercise humility and courtesy. Unless they are professional missionaries, they do not attempt to proselytize by argument at all, but by personal example. When you encounter a person with deep and loving faith, you want to be like that person.

The first believers embraced Christianity not because it was persuasive, but because it was a gift—a surprise no one had predicted or even imagined until it happened. Christianity has never lost that compelling attraction. By definition, the gospel is good news that will be as good today and tomorrow as it was two thousand years ago. As a journalist, I am humbled by the knowledge that yesterday's newspaper is good only for wrapping cold ashes from the fireplace to pitch into the trash. But the good news that undergirds your faith will always be fresh. You will grow old, but the gospel will always be young.

People became Christians because they needed and wanted what Christianity offered, which explains why the earliest Christians were willing to die for their faith. For them, faith was life itself. That fervor is difficult to appreciate today, when religious faith is treated as an option—something to take or leave depending on whether one is inclined to be "religious" or not. We have reached this casual stage because our secular culture has absorbed Christian values without acknowledging their origin in Christian faith. Ironically, indifferent Americans enjoy the social advantages of Christianity free of the burden of personal commitment.

A Victim of Its Own Success

This phenomenon is more pronounced in England, where barely four percent of the queen's subjects worship regularly in the established Church, despite the fact that Christian instruction is required in the nation's tax-supported schools, and Anglican bishops sit by right in the British Parliament. England is now dotted with empty and redundant churches, because its people have absorbed Christianity too well. They are arguably the most civilized people on earth, precisely because Christianity did such an effective job of civilizing them.

The average Englishman no longer feels impelled to worship—not because God is a stranger, but because God is so familiar. The spire of the village church is still the symbol of all that is good about the English spirit, but the people have retained faith in the symbol alone. Happily, however, there are signs of a change of heart. The immense outpouring of emotion that greeted the death of the late Princess Diana impressed the world but surprised the English most of all. In the former days of the empire, England tempered its arrogance with Christian compassion for the less fortunate. Of a sudden, a century later, touched by the princess' impulse to do good, the

English are discovering that they still have Christian hearts.

In many Western nations today Christianity is a victim of its own success. Every aspect of contemporary life—from law and literature to sportsmanship, social service, and justice—reflects our common faith without acknowledging its source or requiring individual commitment. Even people's unthinking *attitudes* are Christian. America, for example, is a nation motivated by volunteerism, generosity, and equal opportunity. To appreciate our progress, look to pagan Rome or to contemporary Saudi Arabia. Just as a fish is unaware of the water in which it swims (because water is its total environment), so our Christian culture is as invisible and as pervasive as the air surrounding us that fills our lungs and sustains our lives. If you seek confirmation of your faith, just look around you.

What many of your friends lack is not Christianity but confidence in the source of beliefs and attitudes they hold in common with you. They have long since unwrapped the gift of faith, hope, and love they share with you, but they have forgotten the giver. C. S. Lewis once compared faith to the sun which, when viewed directly, blinds us, but by whose light we are able to see everything else in the world. We do not yet see God face to face but by his reflection in this world. It is sufficient to give us confidence.

What Christianity Offered That Was New

To grasp Christianity's attractiveness to people two millennia ago, you must return mentally to a time when our faith was an utter novelty. Christianity clearly offered something incomparably better than the lives these people then knew and the prospects held out for them.

To ancient societies segregated by class distinctions, Christianity offered *equality*. Nothing could be more democratic than a faith based on every man, woman, and child being held equally precious by the Creator and worthy of being redeemed by his Son. In place of cold law and cruel punishment, Christianity made *love* the fundamental motive of both God and humans. Whereas ancient peoples despaired of a future, Christianity offered them *hope*. At a time when life seemed aimless, senseless, and tragic, Christianity invested it with victorious *purpose*. Of a sudden, a cold and impersonal universe was demonstrated to be *personal* and *providential*. In place of oblivion, Christianity offered an *eternity* of fulfillment.

Where ancient peoples saw only their limitations, Christianity offered *perfection*—not just the spirit's escape from the prison of the body, but *wholeness* of body and spirit in a *New Creation*. When the only gods pagans knew were distant and fickle, Christianity offered *intimacy* with a *caring* Creator—the only God. Christianity replaced ignominy with *glory*, uncertainty with *confidence*; isolation with *community*, and decay with *transformation*. The new faith offered not only a persuasive explanation for the misery of humanity, but offered *forgiveness* for sin, the triumph of *good* over evil, and *deliverance*. To people who coveted wealth and power, Christianity proclaimed the common virtues of *poverty* and *peacemaking*. Above all, it offered a Savior who, although God's Son, fully shared our human life and its trials, dying for love of *every one of us*.

Today, all who live in a Christian culture, regardless of whether they believe or even acknowledge its source, take this legacy for granted. As democracy and human rights have spread to nations that are not traditionally Christian, their citizens benefit from Christian values as well.

Make no mistake: two thousand years after the good news was first proclaimed, the alternatives to Christian faith are no more attractive than the condition of the pagan Romans before they received the gospel from the provincial Jew, Paul. The alternative to Christian hope is to believe that you have no purpose and no prospects other than those of your own devising.

Alternatives to Faith

The alternative to faith is to maintain that nothing that is was created, but that our universe and everything in it (including ourselves) "just happened." However, evolution itself demonstrates that even dumb nature has purpose, and all people clearly attempt to work their way through life toward goals. The awful alternative to religious faith is to admit that we are only fooling ourselves every time we make a decision. Short of faith, ultimately nothing matters.

Although the truth of your Christian faith cannot be fully demonstrated, neither can the truth of its alternatives, and they have nothing superior to offer. Indeed, what they promise is hopelessness, which explains why atheists are not motivated to become missionaries! Atheists can be mischievous critics, though, because they enjoy the advantage of revealing how Christianity has managed to muddle its legacy of faith over the course of twenty centuries. Because God has been misrepresented on occasion by Christians as a kind of celestial Scrooge, atheists protest that we are enslaved rather than liberated by faith. Because some Christians pretend to know the mind of God and justify unchristian behavior in the name of faith, atheists cry "hypocrites!" Despite the fact that all humans are confused and inconsistent, atheists prefer human judgment to God's—or at least they prefer their own judgment to that of the Church.

The only effective person to dispute an atheist is a saint, because saints admit the errors of Christians and prefer not to argue with anyone. They have nothing to prove. Instead, they love their antagonists and beg their forgiveness. Nothing is more persuasive than a Christian who lives his or her faith quietly, serenely, and fully.

Chesterton remarked that skeptics reject Christianity out of hand as a solution because they fail to appreciate the problem that people cannot live without meaning, hope, or a sense of reality.

Along these lines, there is perhaps no better apologist for our faith than Blaise Pascal, a seventeenth-century Frenchman who attempted an "Apology for the Christian Religion" during his brief life, but died before his random notes could take the form of a book. Subsequently, those bits and pieces of wisdom were collected in *Pensees* (Thoughts), which has become a classic of world literature.

The Wager

Pascal constructed his case for Christianity on the twin foundations of our common experiences and aspirations. "The misery of man without God" is apparent, he declared, adding that human nature is faulty and fickle, a fact "proved by nature itself." Equally true, Pascal claimed, is "the happiness of man with God. That there is a Redeemer is proved by Scripture."

The devout Frenchman acknowledged that humankind's desperation cannot itself demonstrate God's existence, so he proposed a practical wager that goes like this: if you believe in God and there is, indeed, a God, you win eternal happiness. If, on the other hand, you believe in God and he turns out to be a mere figment of your imagination, you lose nothing. But if you reject belief in God, and God exists, you lose for all eternity. Pascal's conclusion: the only losers are those who reject God.

Here is what I suggested about Pascal's wager in my first book, *Growing in Faith*. I can't improve on it:

> *Gambling on God has never attracted me. It assumes that the object of faith is to cash in on an eternal payoff. Moreover, Pascal's wager assumes that God punishes people who, for*

whatever reason, lack faith. That will not do either. But give Pascal his due. He was writing at a time when Christian living involved great sacrifices, and when those who turned from religion did so to pursue lives of sensuality and corruption. Pascal was simply reassuring people who believed in God that they should bet on doing God's will.

Let's take the worst case scenario. Suppose when your life ends that's all there is. First off, you won't realize the loss, because there will no longer be a "you" to experience it. Granted, that does not justify your having lived a life of self-deception. But look at it this way: believing and loving as a Christian is its own reward. It is a good, wise, and sane way to pass through life. You are not likely to have your life shortened by being persecuted and martyred for your faith. On the other hand, you will have the satisfaction of living a responsible, directed life of love and service.

I do not expect to lose Pascal's wage, but my Christian faith is not just a bet on an afterlife. Rather, I am betting on a God who sent his Son to live this life with us and to transform you and me in the process. That is no pipedream.

Does God Exist?

Pascal had a point. Experience teaches us that we are insufficient unto ourselves. Whether or not we are actually miserable, we are clearly incapable of realizing our ultimate aspirations on our own, and we are certain to die. Throughout our lives, we constantly reach beyond our grasp, yearning for transcendence.

We cannot help but wish upon a star; *but is that star God*? Saint Augustine thought so. "Our hearts are restless until they rest in Thee," he professed in his *Confessions* over fifteen centuries ago. God is truth itself, the saint insisted, and truth attracts the human mind, which is distracted only by the sinful will, which settles for much less. Once our wills are healed by Christ's grace, our minds are freed to attain to the God of truth. For Augustine, God's existence is proved by our yearning for him.

Anselm of Canterbury (d. 1109) built on Augustine's inward-looking affirmation. Because God is "a being than which nothing greater can be conceived," and we can conceive of such a being, God's very perfection demands that he exist, Anselm argued.

Taking an entirely different tack, Thomas Aquinas (d. 1274) maintained that God's existence can be proved by external evidence. From the knowledge of our senses, he claimed, we can infer the existence of an immaterial world. Aquinas proposed five approaches to prove God's existence:

1. Because things move, there must be a Prime Mover who set everything in motion.
2. Because nothing happens that is not caused, there must be a First Cause for every subsequent effect.
3. Because all creatures and things are contingent, there must be Something Necessary on which they depend for their existence.
4. Because everything in creation is more or less perfect or imperfect, there must be an Absolute Living Standard of Perfection by which they are judged.
5. Because the universe operates coherently and consistently, there must be an Intelligent Designer.

How persuasive are these "proofs" for God's existence? When I agonized with doubt for years in my late teens and twenties, I confess that Aquinas's arguments left me cold. He still required a leap of faith from our experience to what it infers. Scientists today even cast doubt on Aquinas's premises, noting that the universe is full of randomness and unpredictability. Moreover, just because we think we see causality at work, who's to say it points *beyond* nature? The fact that "b" typically follows "a" does not prove that "a" is the cause of "b." As for perfection, even nonscientists claim that it is not an objective standard at all, but a mere matter of taste.

Even if Aquinas was correct, at best he only demonstrated the existence of a cold and aloof celestial mechanic, not the God of Abraham, Moses, Jesus—and ourselves. There is evidence that Aquinas himself came around to this way of thinking because, on his deathbed, face to face with God in a mystical experience, he dismissed his lifetime of theology as mere "straw."

As for Anselm's argument, I couldn't buy the notion that God must exist simply because I can conceive of a Perfect Being. Moreover, perfection wasn't what I was seeking anyway. In retrospect, I realize that I was looking for a God who loves me, and the only one who can prove that such a being exists was God himself. I sympathized with Augustine, because my heart, too, felt empty and restless. Despairing of demonstrating "the presence of a hidden God" by reason alone, Pascal left it to God to prove *himself* to us by entering human history and our individual lives. Jesus is the proof we have been given.

Ultimately, confident Christians are persuaded of God's existence by the accounts in Scripture and by the person of Jesus. God does not need our affirmation to prove his existence; he has literally imposed himself on us.

Still, not everyone hankers after God. Pascal noted that, for many reasons:

> *Men despise religion, they hate it and fear to find it true. To cure this, I must begin by showing that religion is not contrary to reason—is venerable—inspire respect for it; next, render it attractive; make good men wish it were true, and then show that it is true. Venerable, because it knows man; attractive, because it promises the true good.*

Conflicting Faiths

You won't find many people denying God because they have a grudge against him. They *dis*believe not because they are enemies of faith at all, but because they hold conflicting faiths. A secular humanist's primary faith is in humanity, a communist's is in society. Belief in God strikes them as infidelity to humanity and society. Equally, the scientist's fundamental faith is in the report of his senses and the operation of his intellect. To admit to the possibility of something more only confuses the scientist's enterprise. The sensualist's fundamental faith is in self-gratification; to maintain faith in God as well would expose him to his Creator's censure, so the sensualist confines his faith to himself and his pleasures.

You cannot get through a day without small acts of faith that things will go as expected and that others can be counted on. In this respect, everyone is a believer. If we doubted everything we cannot prove beyond a shadow of a doubt, no one could navigate from sunrise to sunset. The scientist can no more prove that truth extends only as far as his experiments than the Christian can prove the existence of a world the senses cannot reach. But the scientist persists through faith. And the humanist, communist, and sensualist cannot prove that their faiths "work," but that does not deter them. They are not opposed to faith at all, but only to faith in *Someone* who makes demands on them. Everyone makes leaps of faith; but when Christians leap, they find themselves in God's lap.

Happily, it is entirely possible to believe in ourselves, in society, in enjoyment, and in science, while maintaining faith in God. But to juggle multiple faiths takes humility and prioritizing, because we Christians acknowledge that we do not belong to ourselves but to our God. Your faith in God ultimately must take precedence over your other faiths.

Some people, rejecting submission to God, turn against him and become enemies of religion altogether.

During the Enlightenment, Voltaire (d. 1778) mocked Christianity as superstitious in practice but still believed that a reasonable religion was possible. But his fellow philosophers Denis Diderot (d. 1784) and David Hume (d. 1776) insisted that it is impossible to reason one's way to faith, and that religion was fundamentally frivolous.

In the nineteenth century, religion's critics went further, insisting that faith in God was both silly and dangerous. Marx called faith an "opiate," Freud an "illusion," Nietzsche a "repression." They were enraged by what they believed to be religion's opposition to human freedom and progress. To their way of thinking, religion deserved to be not only discounted but destroyed. Forced to choose between God and humanity, they chose humanity (or more precisely, they chose their own judgment).

Nietzsche proclaimed the death of God. In the midst of the nineteenth century's unbridled capitalism and greed, he announced that God himself had become extinct in Darwin's survival-of-the-fittest jungle world. To maintain the Christian ethic in such a world, he argued, was hypocritical, intellectually lazy, and evasive. It was pointless to indulge in the comfort of faith when no one paid attention to God. Better, he advised, for nominal Christians to dispense with the deity altogether, acknowledge that they had tasted and enjoyed the forbidden fruit, and act as gods unto themselves independent of the illusion of religion.

In the twentieth century, Nietzsche's brand of man-is-god thinking drew us into two world wars and produced the Gulag and the Holocaust. By pretending to replace God with themselves, recent generations abandoned their humanity and taught us a lesson: that faith is preferable to irreligion. But which faith is worthy of us?

Religion and Religions

The foundation of all religion is our sense of the *holy* or *sacred*, eliciting *awe* or *reverence*, and developing into *ritual* and *moral observance*. All religions rest on faith, whether their tenets are explicit or only implicit; and all foster a *community* of faith. Although specific beliefs differ from one faith to another, there can be no religion without a human *response* to the sacred. God is not religious; *we* are!

In Europe during the Middle Ages, there was no demarcation between secular and religious life; religion was integral to daily living, thinking, and feeling. A similar situation exists today for the Hindus of India, the Buddhists of Tibet, and some tribal societies. For them, religion and daily living are synonymous. By contrast, we Christians have lived concurrently in secular and religious worlds since the Renaissance.

You will often hear the casual cliché that "all religions are basically the same" as a way of dismissing them all. That cliche is correct only in the sense that all faiths are alike in acknowledging the sacred. The corollary that "there is truth in all religions" is correct only in the sense that peoples, regardless of their faith, are realistic when they respond to the sacred. Irreligion, on the other hand, is false because it is blind to ultimate reality.

But the "truth" common to all religions is easily overstated. For example, I suspect that you would prefer no faith at all to a religion that calls for human sacrifice and cannibalism!

The real differences between faiths become more pronounced where they are in competition. Religions seldom compete these days, but adherents employ their faiths from time to time as weapons of righteousness against one another, as in the contemporary Middle East and in Africa. In Northern Ireland, Christianity itself remains riven because of the animosity of Protestants and Catholics. Some fanatics are not satisfied unless they are fighting a holy war.

All religions satisfy the deep-seated human need to find meaning in life and to find a community that shares and sustains that meaning. Strictly speaking, there are no "infidels" among religious peoples, but only men and women who hold to differing religious faiths. They all deserve our respect.

In what sense, then, is Christianity "right" and other faiths "wrong?" The answer is: only in the total *content* of faith—not in its *practice*. A good Jew, a faithful Moslem, a devout Hindu, or a dedicated Buddhist is truly religious and infinitely more pleasing to God than an indifferent Christian. What Christianity alone claims is that God has revealed more to us than these other faiths possess—most notably in the life, death, and resurrection of God's Son, his victory over death, the availability of grace and forgiveness, and the prospect of eternity.

That is why Christianity is a missionary religion: it cannot and must not keep the good news of the gospel to itself. Its success across vastly divergent cultures attests equally to the religious aspirations common to all peoples and to the great expectations Christianity holds out to everyone.

Saint Augustine, in his *Confessions*, insisted that, just as there is but one God, there is but one true religion:

> *. . . expressed outwardly and carried on under one set of names and signs in the past and (under) another set now; it was more secret then and more open now . . . yet it is one and the same true religion . . . The saving grace of this religion, the only true one, through which alone true salvation is truly promised, has never been refused to anyone who was worthy of it.*

That is the faith you enjoy and in which you will find confidence.

The Advantages of Christianity

Among the great world religions Christianity is at once more gracious and more realistic than its fellow faiths—

gracious in its appreciation of God, realistic in its assessment of human nature. By contrast, Judaism and Islam are essentially *ethical* religions, which lay out disciplines for believers to follow to prove their fidelity. Follow the rules and observances, and God will be faithful to you, they proclaim. Flout them, and you bring down condemnation on your heads.

Considering that Judaism formed the historical foundation of Christianity, and that Mohammed based Islam on elements of the two older faiths, you might expect substantial similarities among the three religions. But, unlike its fellow faith, Christianity is not based on ethical submission or ritual observance. Rule-keeping and church attendance in themselves do not make one a *good* Christian.

In fact, Christians are loath to call anyone good, because goodness is one's likeness to God, and that can be discerned in the human heart by God alone. As you know, Christianity recognizes no *living* saints, but only those who have already passed through life and gone to God. Christianity is realistic about human nature, acknowledging that the best of us are flawed and fallible. Just as alcoholics remain alcoholics even when they stop drinking, Christians remain sinners even when they aren't sinning.

As I mentioned in my last letter, Jesus calls you and me to be perfect like his heavenly Father. That means that goodness is something other than righteousness; rather, it is *God-likeness*, which is less a religious regimen than it is a transformation of one's spirit. When at last you see God face to face, what do you think *he* will see in you? He will discern the likeness to himself that he originally made part of your design when he gave you life.

Christianity is not only more realistic about human nature than other faiths are, but more appreciative of God's nature. We recognize God to be not only our Creator and Sustainer, but our Redeemer and our Destiny. In his Son, God bent down to become one of us, to share the pain, sorrows, uncertainties, and anxieties of human life, and to die to accomplish what we cannot manage for ourselves—to replace our selfishness with God's selflessness, to forgive our sins, to unlock eternity, and to save us from ourselves.

In the practice of their faiths, Jews and Moslems often put Christians to shame, but we Christians have more to work with and more to aspire to if we will only accept the gifts of God.

Christianity's contrast to the great Eastern faiths is even more pronounced. Neither Hinduism nor Buddhism conceives of a creating and sustaining God, let alone a redeeming, loving, and forgiving divinity and an eternal source of human hope. Still, the Eastern faiths possess an pervasive sense of the sacredness of life and a capacity for reverence that largely eludes the more literal-minded Western religions. For both Hinduism and Buddhism, however, salvation is elusive and consists of escaping reality rather than engaging and embracing it. By contrast, Christians are never more *alive* than when we confront our Creator.

Obstacles to Faith

To achieve confidence, you will have to confront your own doubts and meet new challenges to your faith. For example, a century ago evolution was trumpeted as disproving Christianity once and for all. But, over time, many Christians have not only come to accept Darwin's theory, but believe that it exemplifies the manner in which God works. Where once it was popularly argued that humans descended from the apes, scientists now have a much richer sense of humankind's distinctiveness as well as the complexity of evolutionary forces. If anything, the theory of physical evolution suggests that God has never taken leave of his creation, and that life is not static but has purpose.

Similarly, science was once considered religion's enemy, whereas we now appreciate that science and faith are only two ways of knowing reality. At its best, science answers the question "how?" while religion responds to the question "why?" Both science and religion also answer the question "what?" from different but compatible points of view. An individual scientist may choose to dismiss religious faith as irrelevant to the practice of his profession, but no sensible Christian will dismiss science as a source of knowledge.

Scientists who reject faith have no scientific basis for doing so, just as no person of faith has a religious basis for denying science. Recall that St. Augustine defined God as the truth; assuming the saint was correct, then all truth, however derived, is divine. At the same time, science, although sure of its methods, is increasingly tentative in its pronouncements. To their chagrin, whole populations have been told that certain foods and chemicals are destructive to their health, only to hear a few years later that new evidence has changed the researchers' minds. Clearly, humility is not a virtue that applies to religious people alone!

At one time, the divisions among Christians were lodged against Christianity's claim to truth. But our faith's diversity is increasingly viewed as confirmation of its vitality and proof of its perennial pull on the spirit of humankind. The rise of the ecumenical movement in the twentieth century demonstrates that we Christians seek unity in diversity. Despite denominational differences, we all embrace a common core of revelation and the same good news. If anything, the adherence of Protestant, Catholic, and Orthodox Christians to their individual traditions is an expression of their reverence for special gifts.

Fortunately, religion's ancient animosities and righteous self-congratulation are in retreat; the Christian wars of faith have ended in an armistice that looks very much like peace. All Christians worship but one God, and it is Jesus' prayer that all Christians be one. The sin of disunity reflects not at all on God, but on ourselves. It is a spur to humility.

More recent challenges to our faith stem from the tendency of celebrity scholars to rush into popular print with their latest "discoveries" of myth in the Bible and their doubts about sayings attributed to Jesus. Traditionally, the quest for the historical Jesus was pursued by reputable scholars who submitted their theories for peer review before publication. Today, sensing commercial interest, some scholars express their views, unchallenged by fellow professionals, in magazines available at the supermarket checkout counter. Their motive is vanity and money, not Christian enlightenment.

Psychological Obstacles

As Christianity enters its third millennium, the most potent challenges to your faith may be subjective. Over the course of the twentieth century, the world has tried other ideologies, and they have all failed. Although there are really no attractive alternatives to faith, there persists a pervasive uncertainty that stems from a sense of our aloneness in the universe, and from a heightened awareness of how badly people treat one another.

Before Copernicus, the universe seemed to be just large enough to display the grandeur of God, and just compact enough to make us feel at home at its center. When we discovered that the universe does not, in fact, revolve around us, that fact alone seemed to diminish our importance in God's scheme. In recent decades, we have landed on the moon and sent out probes through the solar system in initial efforts to explore the universe. But instead of confirming our genius, these successful adventures have left many people bewildered by the vastness and emptiness of space, and fearful of the fires of countless stars and the annihilating power of black holes.

Despite Einstein's reassurances to the contrary, many of your contemporaries sense that relativity has made everything relative. Where can we find God in endless space? And where is our privileged place in God's creation if, as many suspect, there are other intelligent beings in the universe?

There was a time not so long ago when people truly *feared* God—not his punishment, but his power and majesty. Remember that religion began with awe. When God sent his Son to become one of us, he did not thereby shrink himself to human size. God is still awesome. Some Christians seek comfort and consolation in him, wanting a kind of divine Santa Claus—but God has never been that. Christian confidence must rest in the Creator who made the sun, the moon, the stars, and even black holes. Our God does not seek to frighten you with these immensities, but only to astound you with his sense of adventure. He plays on the largest stage and on the grandest scale.

Many persons are appalled by the apparent waste in nature—so much life, and over so soon. But from God's point of view, this is simply abundance. Life springs from death, and life goes on. We might feel more comfortable cast as players in a one-set drawing room comedy; instead, you and I find ourselves in a titanic spectacle with a cast of billions. That fact can be unsettling unless you consider the reliability of our Set Designer and Director. From God's point of view, no man, woman, or child has a bit part in the play of life. Each of us enjoys top billing.

If, indeed, there are other intelligent creatures in the universe, they belong to God no less than we do. Remember, there were angels before there were men and women. Would you deny God the enjoyment of making other creatures destined to be happy with him?

As a young child, I was frightened of bridges and skyscrapers, and intimidated by adults and strangers. It is only natural, of course, for children to feel small and helpless, because that is what they are. But as adults, we learn to appreciate the immensity of God's imagination, and even to relish the unexpected as a foretaste of the endless adventure that eternity will be in the company of our Creator.

Suffering as an Impediment to Faith

Marilyn vos Savant, credited by the *Guinness Book of World Records* as being the brightest person in the world, was once asked whether the world would be better off if all suffering and misery could be eliminated. She hedged her reply, noting in *Parade* magazine: "In a culture that is so sensitive to the teensiest discomfort and inconvenience that we invent things like heated stadium cushions and revolving tie racks, I don't think we'd have a problem finding plenty about which to be unhappy."

Our urge to either blame God for human suffering or to deny his existence because of the persistence of human misery has waned in the past century. As a journalist, I am inclined to credit my profession for this change in public attitude. Newspapers and television make it abundantly clear that most human misery is self-imposed or is inflicted by one human being on another. Consider that we have just endured a century of total war, with worldwide suffering and atrocities on a scale not previously known. God was not to blame; people were.

Neither is God involved in random accidents that leave human victims, nor in the devastation caused when nature acts according to its laws. We may curse water when it floods and drowns, fire when it burns, volcanoes when they erupt, and wind when it destroys property. But human intelligence equips us to deal with natural forces, if not always to control them, then at least to evade them. Jesus himself warned about the fragility of houses built on sand, so we do best to insure ourselves against accidents and natural tragedies.

If some people live in want, it is because the rest of us allow it. If a plane falls from the sky, it is because it was badly designed, maintained, or flown. Are you as impressed as I am that people who suffer tragedy do not blame or deny God because of their misfortunes? Instead, they typically thank God that their losses weren't worse and ask his help in rebuilding their health, their homes, and their lives.

Admittedly, physical and mental pain and decline are something else altogether. Chronic pain is senseless and debilitating. As Christians, we believe that death is but the portal to eternity; but when many Americans die, they are no longer themselves, but only hollow shells containing little of the persons we knew. Granted, medicine could do a better job of pain management, but why does God stand by while his own creatures fail?

The best answer I know is that God has been through this before, when he denied his Son's plea that he be delivered from torture and crucifixion. Human Redemption was accomplished by God's own pain and death. That does not mean that all pain is redemptive, but it does suggest that our transformation into creatures worthy of happiness with our Creator still involves suffering. People often ask me what words a Christian should use to console a person in pain. My answer is that Christianity is a hopeful faith, but not an especially comforting one. What we can do is to imitate Christ in his generous acceptance of suffering.

As Marilyn vos Savant wryly noted, we are inclined to treat even minor discomfort as pain, and to complain about anything short of nirvana. The persistence of drug abuse demonstrates the human insistence on instant and carefree bliss. In reality, some suffering appears to be an unavoidable part of the human condition. Fortunately, we possess Jesus' example of putting pain to good use.

Capturing Confidence

There was a time not so long ago when people respected age not just in wine and antiques, but in people. We revered our elders not because they had lived faultless lives, but because they had survived their mistakes and possessed a wisdom to impart to us. Today, people are more inclined to consigning their elders to nursing homes rather than listening to them.

In place of experience, many people prefer novelty, not least because youth is vital, and new fashions in ideas have not had the time to reveal their flaws. When Christianity appeared two millennia ago, it was a captivating novelty. Two thousand years later, we acknowledge that plenty of mistakes have been made in the name of faith. Over the years, the Church and its people have twisted the Sermon on the Mount to justify war, violence, bigotry, and lies. Lust for power and pleasure have found refuge under the mantle of religion and, even now, there are places where the Church of Christ is infested with bureaucrats more committed to budgets and spreadsheets than to devotion.

But these persistent flaws only illustrate that we Christians have been redeemed but not yet transformed. Our beliefs have not been tried and found wanting; they have yet to be tried. I pray you will try them.

Despite the abuses of believers, the gospel is the same good news uttered by the mouth of Jesus in Galilee. Our Redeemer still lives, and will live through endless tomorrows. Despite our sins, you and I are loved and are hopeful. Through God's amazing grace, you will dispel doubt, grow in faith, exult in our common hope, and live in love.

All it takes is a little confidence.

Faithfully,

Your father

Notes and Acknowledgments

I am not altogether confident that my daughters have completely read these lengthy letters as yet, but I am satisfied to have written them before I got much older. They are love letters, and love is its own justification.

Out of respect for their privacy, I have not revealed much about my offspring in these pages, but you deserve to know something about them and what they have been through. All three women were born with moderate to severe learning disabilities. Virginia, now thirty-three, suffered grand mal seizures as an infant and was deaf for nearly a year. Through faith, grit, and the devotion of my wife (their stepmother), she and her twin sisters (now thirty) graduated from college as honor students. Doctors and teachers predicted that Virginia would not be able to cope outside an institutional setting, but she leads an independent and self-supporting life.

As a young child, Lisa was functionally sightless in one eye. Today, she is a graduate of the prestigious Corcoran School of Art and an accomplished artist and photographer. Her twin, Christina, worked her way through graduate school to become a social worker, and has helped the homeless, AIDS victims and their families, and the addicted. Every day she gives comfort and confidence to people whose hope is flagging.

All three women have prevailed over permanent handicaps that might have drained their lives of confidence altogether.

There is nothing proprietary about faith, hope, and love, so I am pleased that these letters now have readers beyond my family—and my daughters are pleased to share them with you. As each of them can attest, life is tough to negotiate in any circumstance. You, too, deserve to live confidently.

Librarians will doubtless shelve this book alongside its predecessor, *Growing in Faith*, under the category of "apologetics," which is the defense of religion. But in both books, I have tried to be neither defensive nor argumentative. Christianity's strengths have been manifest over two millennia and do not require another author to rally the troops with the old cry, "Onward, Christian soldiers!"

Nor have I attempted to *persuade* you of the truth of the faith, but only to clear away some rubble from the path to conviction, and to affirm that confidence in Christianity is not misplaced. No one but God could have invented Christianity—or even imagined it—yet our faith is manifestly plausible.

Religious skepticism too often masquerades as intellectual humility, when it is only vanity—an aversion to any truth but one's own. I believe it unlikely that God would create creatures in his own likeness, only to leave them in the dark about his intentions and their destiny.

In any case, faith is a gift. If Christianity could be proven beyond the shadow of a doubt, there would still be room for indifference. Confident Christians reject indifference once and for all, while acknowledging that their faith must coexist with doubt until they are taken up into the New Creation.

Taken together, these letters comprise my fifth book in as many years. This one has been the hardest yet to bring off, because it is addressed to my children, who have every reason to be my most astute critics. Moreover, as I wrote, I sensed the spirits of Lewis, Chesterton, and Merton peering over my shoulder and muttering "tsk, tsk" when I fell short of their standards. I can only hope that this book inspires my readers to explore the writings of these masters. Specifically, I trust that my chapters on miracles and the New Creation accurately reflect Lewis's own thinking, expressed in his book entitled *Miracles*.

I am grateful to other authors as well. The chapter on Jesus was enriched by my reading of Philip Yancey's *The*

Jesus I Never Knew and Luke Timothy Johnson's *The Real Jesus*. My account of the New Testament was aided by Tom Wright's *What Saint Paul Really Said*. For the chapter on the Church I relied heavily on David Christie-Murray's *A History of Heresy*. Bruno Bettelheim's *The Uses of Enchantment* inspired my chapter on magic. Homer Rogers' *Uncommon Sense* helped me with the account of the New Creation, and Bill Wilson's compilation of *The Best of Josh McDowell* gave me an appreciation of the lines of argument taken by contemporary Christian apologists, even as I chose to stray from some of them.

When I embarked on this book, I had just read Paul Johnson's *The Quest for God*. While I am unaware of borrowing anything from that historian's personal profession of faith, I am grateful for his inspiration. I did lean heavily on Johnson's *A History of the Jews* and *A History of Christianity* for my chapters on the Bible and the Law, however. Throughout, I am indebted to J. B. Phillips's clear and compelling translation of the New Testament.

Thanks to my editors, Jeremy Langford and Kass Dotterweich, as well as marketing director Tom Hoffman and designers Kathy Kikkert and GrafixStudio, Inc., for believing in the book and seeing it into print, a process that took considerably longer than God's creation of the universe. Thanks, too, to Peter Copeland, editor of my syndicated column, "Amazing Grace," and to Liz Lockhart, producer-director of the cable television program I host in Northern Virginia. Both help to anchor my feet to the ground when my head is in the heavens. Preparing a newspaper column and hosting a weekly program on contemporary Christianity, far from distracting me from my writing, helps me to affirm that a faith now two thousand years old is as fresh, new, and relevant as today's sunrise.

Thanks to my fellow Quakers, who inspire me and live up to their name—Friends—and to the Gideons, for their help in negotiating the Bible.

And a special note of gratitude to the member institutions of the Washington Theological Consortium—twelve Catholic and Protestant seminaries I am honored to serve as vice-chairman. I am honored to witness ecumenism firsthand.

Most of all, I am indebted to my wife, Becky (a popular author herself), for insisting that the text be practical and reader friendly, and for alerting me to times when I am too confident for my own good. She, like my faith, is a precious gift from God, and I give thanks to him for her.

If you have comments about this book, I would appreciate hearing from you. Write me c/o P.O. Box 2758, Woodbridge, VA 22193 or dyount@erols.com. I also invite you to visit me on the Internet at www.erols.com/dyount.

David Yount
Montclair, Virginia
Fathers Day 2000

BIBLIOGRAPHY

It wasn't until I reached college that I fully realized that cramming for an exam with *Cliff's Notes* didn't rank with reading the real thing. Christians seeking to strengthen their faith do best to read the classics. Commentaries such as this one are only secondary references. Why read a book *about* Shakespeare when you can read the Bard himself? Not because the original is heavy going—classics typically earn their reputation because they are well-written. Notably, no one makes friends with the authors of textbooks, but it is a thrill to read St. Augustine in his own words as he grapples with his own beliefs, doubts, and emotions. He is one of my companions in faith and can be yours.

Here are a few personal favorites:

Saint Augustine. *Confessions* (Doubleday Image, 1958)
G. K. Chesterton. *Orthodoxy* (Doubleday Image, 1958)
Thomas Merton. *The Seven Storey Mountain* (Harcourt, Brace Jovanovitch, 1948)
C. S. Lewis. *Mere Christianity* (Macmillan, 1943)
Blaise Pascal. *Pensees* (many editions in English)

On the whole, recent books of apologetics leave much to be desired. Many are written in an "us-versus-them" adversarial style, dismissing skepticism out of hand when, in fact, doubt is ever the companion of faith. Moreover, some apologists tend to treat the Bible as its own self-verifying universe. A few authors claim to actually *prove* the truth of Christianity, when at most they only demonstrate its credibility.

Over a lifetime, the confident Christian will meet plenty of people who could be persuaded of Christianity's credibility, but who have their own reasons for not wanting to submit to faith. Ironically, some popular defenders of the faith tend to think of their unbelieving "opponents" as sophisticated and rational atheists, when most are only self-centered and indifferent agnostics who yawn at religion.

Here are some of the better popular books I consulted:

Campolo, Tony. *A Reasonable Faith* (Word, 1983)
Gerstner, John H. *Reasons for Faith* (Soli Deo Gloria, 1995)
Guest, John. *In Search of Certainty* (Regal Books, 1983)
Harpur, John. *The Thinking Person's Guide to God* (Prima, 1996)
Johnson, Paul. *The Quest for God* (HarperCollins, 1996)
Johnson, Phillip E. *Reason in the Balance* (InterVarsity, 1995)
Kennedy, D. James. *Skeptics Answered* (Multnomah Books, 1997)
McGrath, Alister E. *Intellectuals Don't Need God and Other Myths* (Zondervan, 1993)
Palau, Luis. *God Is Relevant* (Doubleday, 1997)
Sproul, R. C. *If There's a God, Why Are There Atheists?* (Tyndale House, 1974)
Sproul, R. C., John Herstner and Arthur Lindsley, *Classical Apologetics* (Academe Books, 1984)

The following books are heavier going but worth the effort:

Baum, Gregory. "A Modern Apologetics." *Faith and Doctrine: A Contemporary View* (Newman Press, 1969)
Burrell, David. *Knowing the Unknowable God* (University of Notre Dame Press, 1986)
Caporale, Rocco, and Antonio Grumelli, eds. *The Culture of Unbelief* (University of California Press, 1971)
Gilkey, Langdon. *Naming the Whirlwind: The Renewal of God-Language* (Bobbs-Merrill, 1986)

Haught, John. *What Is God? How to Think About the Divine* (Paulist Press, 1986)
Kasper, Walter. *The God of Jesus Christ* (Crossroad, 1984)
Kung, Hans. *Does God Exist? An Answer for Today* (Doubleday, 1980)
Marty, Martin. *Varieties of Unbelief* (Doubleday, 1966)
Novak, Michael. *Belief and Unbelief: A Philosophy of Self-Knowledge* (Macmillan, 1965)
Shea, John. *Stories of God: An Unauthorized Biography* (Thomas More, 1978)

Negotiating the Bible

Although the Bible is not self-verifying, it is powerful reading and, I believe, ultimately persuasive. It is, after all, the compendium of God's revelation. The Bible takes itself for granted, and properly so, because God feels no compulsion to prove his own existence. We *are* because he *is*. We do not create him or even find him; he created and found us.

Just as confident Christians pray to get their Creator's attention, they read the Bible to listen to God. In this appendix, I suggest ways to become comfortable with reading Scripture. I suggest starting with Genesis and Exodus to get a sense of God's intentions, then jumping to the Letters of St. Paul, which were written even before the gospel accounts. Paul assumes his readers already believe, but he explains the real-life consequences of their faith better than anyone else. Then read the Gospels themselves to discover the Jesus who encompasses all of God's revelation.

To become confident of the meaning of what you are reading, you may want to seek assistance from a priest, minister, or lay person in theology.

Great Bible Chapters

Creation

The great epic of beginnings: Genesis 1–3

Ten Commandments

As important today as ever: Exodus 20

Moses' farewell
Great themes of Jewish life: Deuteronomy 6

Challenge for Joshua
Stirring words of encouragement and strength: Joshua 1

David's great prayer
A prayer of praise and dedication: 1 Chronicles 29:10–19

The Shepherd's psalm
Most treasured of all psalms: Psalm 23

Psalm of nature
Praising God's creation: Psalm 19

Psalm of praise
Answer of the sheep to the shepherd: Psalm 100

Psalm of salvation
A psalm of thankful memories: Psalm 107

Psalm of God's Word
For those who love God's law: Psalm 119

Proverbs of Wisdom
Good advice for young men and women: Proverbs 3

The Suffering Servant
Isaiah's prophecy of the Messiah: Isaiah 53

Ezekiel's strange vision
Wind, fire, winged creatures: Ezekiel 1

The greatest thing in the world
Paul's chapter on love: 1 Corinthians 13

The secrets of happiness
The source of true contentment and courage: Philippians 4

Great heroes of faith
The Bible's "Hall of Fame": Hebrews 11

The City of God
A new world is coming: Revelation 21, 22

Great Bible Stories

Noah survives a catastrophe
A major rescue operation: Genesis 6, 7, 8

Abraham and Isaac
Abraham's trust in God tested: Genesis 22:1–18

Jacob and Esau
Jacob fooled his father, but not God: Genesis 27:1–46

Joseph's rise to power
A rags-to-riches story: Genesis 37–49

A royal rescue for Moses
God rewards a desperate plan: Exodus 1:7–2:10

Exodus
A nation of slaves freed: Exodus 7–14

Jericho falls
A spy story and a miraculous victory: Joshua 5:10–6:26

The day the sun stood still
God tips the scales: Joshua 10

Deborah to the rescue
Two women show courage and determination: Judges 4

Gideon's strange army
Trumpets and lanterns for weapons: Judges 6, 7

Samson's fame and fall
Israel's strong man couldn't control women: Judges 14–17

Ruth and Boaz
A tender love story: Ruth

The call of Samuel
A mysterious voice in the night: 1 Samuel 3

David's call to destiny
God chooses the youngest son: 1 Samuel 16:1–13

David and Goliath
A young man's faith cannot be beaten: 1 Samuel 17

David and Jonathan
A story of undying loyalty: 1 Samuel 20

David and Saul
Tense moments in a wilderness cave: 1 Samuel 23–24

David and Bathsheba
Sin, tragedy, and repentance: 2 Samuel 11–12

David and Absalom
Treachery and tragedy break a father's heart: 2 Samuel 15–18

The Queen of Sheba
Two monarchs and their riches: 1 Kings 10

Elijah's God outdoes the false prophets
Blazing finish to a long day: 1 Kings 18

Elisha and the general
Strange cure in a dirty river: 2 Kings 5

Josiah's great discovery
Housecleaning in the Temple: 2 Kings 22

Nehemiah's dream come true
The walls of Jerusalem rise again: Nehemiah

Esther's finest hour
A beauty contest and the king's policies: Esther

Job's problems
Why do good people suffer? Job 1–3

The fiery furnace
Three young men come out unharmed: Daniel 3

Daniel's night with the lions
The king learns new respect for Daniel's God: Daniel 6

Jonah's vacation plans backfire
God won't take "no" for an answer: Jonah

Philip and the Ethiopian
African becomes a follower of Christ: Acts 8

Conversion of Saul
Dynamic Jewish leader stopped in his tracks: Acts 9

The Philippian jailer
Earthquake almost leads to jailbreak: Acts 16

Paul's shipwreck
One danger after another: Acts 27–28

Suggested Readings from the Old Testament

The beginning
Genesis 1
The fall of man
Genesis 3
The flood
Genesis 6–8
Abraham tested
Genesis 22
Jacob's dream at Bethel
Genesis 28
The birth of Moses
Exodus 2
Moses and the burning bush
Exodus 3
Manna and quail
Exodus 16
Moses and the glory of the Lord
Exodus 33
Balaam's donkey
Numbers 22
The death of Moses
Deuteronomy 34
The Lord commands Joshua
Joshua 1
Crossing the Jordan
Joshua 3
The fall of Jericho
Joshua 5, 6
Gideon defeats the Midianites
Judges 7
The Lord calls Samuel
1 Samuel 3
David and Goliath
1 Samuel 17

Elijah on Mount Carmel
1 Kings 18
Benefits of Wisdom
Proverbs 3
Sayings of the wise
Proverbs 22
The wife of noble character
Proverbs 31
Remember your Creator while young
Ecclesiastes 11, 12
Isaiah's commission
Isaiah 6
To us a Child is born
Isaiah 9
Comfort for God's people
Isaiah 40
The suffering and glory of the Servant
Isaiah 52, 53
Invitation to the thirsty
Isaiah 55
Jehoiakim burns Jeremiah's scroll
Jeremiah 36
The writing on the wall
Daniel 5
Daniel in the den of lions
Daniel 6

Suggested Readings from the Psalms

The way of righteousness: Psalm 1
A plea of mercy: Psalm 6
The God of creation: Psalm 8
God's witness: Psalm 19
The suffering of the Messiah: Psalm 22
The Shepherd psalm: Psalm 23
Who may ascend the hill of the Lord?: Psalm 24
A plea for pardon: Psalm 25

The Lord is my light and my salvation: Psalm 27
A psalm for forgiveness: Psalm 32
The Lord is good: Psalm 34
The greatness and glory of God: Psalm 48
A psalm of repentance: Psalm 51
He alone is my rock and my salvation: Psalm 62
Longing for God: Psalm 63
Remember the Lord: Psalm 77
How lovely is your dwelling place, O Lord: Psalm 84
Worship and warning: Psalm 95
O worship the Lord: Psalm 96
The praise of a pardoned people: Psalm 103
I love the Lord because he hears me: Psalm 116
A song of the redeemed: Psalm 118
In praise of God's Word: Psalm 119
Where does my help come from?: Psalm 121
Building a house: Psalm: 127
Penitence and pardon: Psalm 130
His love endures forever: Psalm 136
Hear my prayer, O Lord: Psalm 143
Great is the Lord: Psalm 145
Praise the Lord: Psalm 146

Suggested Readings from the New Testament

Jesus rides into Jerusalem
Luke 19:28–48
The Last Supper
Luke 22:1–23
A parting message
John 14:1–21
Jesus arrested
Mark 14:32–56
The trial of Jesus
Mark 15:1–20

Jesus crucified
Luke 23:32–56
The Resurrection
Matthew 28:1–20
The Ascension
Acts 1:1–14
The Holy Spirit comes
Acts 2:1–39
An Ethiopian converted
Acts 8:26–40
Paul converted
Acts 9:1–25
Paul preaches on Mars Hill
Acts 17:16–34
Paul's defense before King Agrippa
Acts 26:1–29
God and sin
Romans 1:16–32
Becoming a Christian
Romans 10:1–17
Faith, wisdom, and perseverance
James 1:1–18
The last days
2 Peter 3:1–18
A New Heaven and a New Earth
Revelation 21:1–27
Jesus is coming soon
Revelation 22:1–21
The Son of God becomes man
John 1:1–18
Jesus Christ is born
Luke 2:1–20
Jesus' childhood
Matthew 2:1–23
Jesus introduced by John the Baptist
Matthew 3:1–17
His life's work begins
Luke 4:1–21

Jesus feeds the five thousand
Mark 6:30–56
Jesus heals the sick and calms the storm
Matthew 8:1–34
Parable of the Sower
Matthew 13:1–23
Parables of the Kingdom of Heaven
Matthew 13:24–52
Parable of the Lost Son
Luke 15:11–32
Parable of the Talents
Luke 19:11–27

What the Bible Teaches about . . .

God

The creation story
"In the beginning, God": Genesis 1
The creation of man
"In the image of God": Genesis 2
A vision of God's holiness
"Holy, holy, holy": Isaiah 6
How God answered Job
"Where were you, Job?": Job 38–41
God without equal
"The greatness of the Creator": Isaiah 40
Psalm of amazement
"What is man?": Psalm 8

Sin and Redemption

The first sin
"Did God say?": Genesis 3
Psalm of confession
"Have mercy on me": Psalm 51
God's promise to his people
"Because the Lord loves you":
Deuteronomy 7:6–8:.10

The Suffering Servant
“Are we like sheep?”: Isaiah 53
Nicodemus at night
“For God so loved the world”: John 3
All have sinned
“The answer is faith”: Romans 3:10–25
The importance of the Resurrection
“Is faith in vain?”: 1 Corinthians 15:1–28
Redemption from the world
“Saved by God’s grace”: Ephesians 2:1–10
The Heavenly City
“Former things have passed away”: Revelation 21, 22

Living in God’s family

The promise to Abraham
“A multitude of nations”: Genesis 17:1–8
God’s New Covenant
“Written upon their hearts”: Jeremiah 31:31–34
The coming of the Spirit
“He will be in you”: John 14:15–31
The Day of Pentecost
“The birth of a church”: Acts 2
Adopted into the family
“From slaves to sons”: Galatians 4:1–7
David at worship
“All is thine”: 1 Chronicles 29:10–22
The early church
“Breaking bread in their homes”: Acts 2:41–47
Meeting together for worship
“Encouraging one another”: Hebrews 10:19–25
Command to baptize
“Teaching and baptizing”: Matthew 28:16–20
Baptized into his death
“Sign of identification”: Romans 6:1–5
The Last Supper
“This is my body”: Matthew 26:20–29

The practice of communion in the churches
"A guide to proper practice":
1 Corinthians 11:17–34

Christian attitudes to the events and crisis of life

Adversity
Matthew 10:28–33
Philippians 4:4–7
Anger
Matthew 5:22–25
James 1:19–21
Citizenship
Matthew 22:21
Romans 12:17 to 13:14
Titus 3:1–6
1 Peter 2:13–17
Contentment
Colossians 3:16–17
Hebrews 13:5–6
Conversation
Ephesians 4:15, 20–32
2 Timothy 2:23–26
Criticism
Matthew 7:1–5
Romans 2:1–4
Romans 14:4–13
Death
John 11:25–27
Romans 14:7–9
Philippians 1:21
1 Thessalonians 4:13–18
Discipleship
John 15:1–8
Acts 11:19–26
1 Peter 2:21–25
Diligence
Romans 12:11
Enemies
Matthew 5:10–12, 43–48
Faith
Mark 11:22–24
Romans 5:1–2
Hebrews 11:1 to 12:2
Faithfulness
Luke 19:12–26
1 Corinthians 4:1–5
Fellowship
Acts 2:42–47
Romans 12:9–16
1 Corinthians 10:16–17
1 John 1:5–7
Forgiveness
Matthew 18:21–35
Acts 13:26–39
Ephesians 4:31–32
Friendship
John 15:12–17
James 4:4
Generosity
Acts 4:34–37
Acts 20:32–35
2 Corinthians 9:6–15
Gratitude
Luke 17:17–18
Colossians 3:15
1 Thessalonians 5:18
Honesty
Romans 12:17
Ephesians 4:28

Humility
Luke 22:24–27
John 13:4–17
Philippians 2:3–11
1 Peter 5:5–7
Jealousy
Luke 15:25–32
Galatians 5:19–26
James 3:13–18
Love
1 Corinthians 13:1–3
1 John 4:7–12
Marriage
Mark 10:2–12
Ephesians 5:21–33
Obedience
Matthew 7:24–29
Matthew 12:50
John 15:10–14
Acts 5:29–32
Old age
Luke 2:25–38
Titus 2:1–6
1 Peter 3:10–12
Patience
James 5:7–11
Permissiveness
Romans 6:1–2, 11–14
1 Corinthians 6:9–20
Prayer
Matthew 26:38–41
Luke 18:1–8
Ephesians 6:18
Priorities
Matthew 6:33
Luke 12:15–21
Purity
2 Timothy 2:22
Titus 1:15–16
Riches
Matthew 6:24, 33
Mark 10:17–31
1 Timothy 6:7–12
Righteousness
Romans 1:16–18
Romans 3:10–26
Romans 5:1–21
Romans 6:11–23
Salvation
Romans 10:9–11
Ephesians 2:4–9
Titus 2:11–14
Steadfastness
Luke 9:51
1 Corinthians 15:57–58
Ephesians 6:10–18
1 Peter 5:8–10
Sympathy
Romans 15:1
Hebrews 13:3
James 1:27
1 Peter 3:8
Thoughts
Romans 12:3
Philippians 4:8

Where to Find Help When . . .

Afraid or fearful
Psalm 34
Psalm 56:3, 4, 10, 11
Isaiah 41:10
Mark 4:35–41
Anxious or worried
Psalm 46
Isaiah 43:1–3
Matthew 6:25–34
Philippians 4:6, 7
Bereaved
Psalm 23
1 Corinthians 15:51–57
1 Thessalonians 4:13–18
Revelation 22:3–5
Bitter or critical
Psalm 73
Matthew 7:1–5
1 Corinthians 13
Choosing a career
Proverbs 31:10–30
Matthew 19:4–6
Ephesians 5:22–33
Conscious of Sin
Psalm 51
Luke 7:36–50
Contemplating marriage
Proverbs 31:10–30
Matthew 19:4–6
Ephesians 5:22–33
Danger threatens
Psalm 91
Proverbs 18:10
Mark 4:37–41
Dedicating your life
Joshua 24:14, 15
Matthew 16:24–26
Romans 12:1, 2
Depressed or discouraged
Romans 8:28–29
2 Corinthians 4:8, 9, 16–18
Hebrews 12:1–3
1 Peter 4:12, 13
Doubting
Mark 9:23, 24
John 20:24–29
Failure comes
Psalm 77
Hebrews 4:14–16
Jude 24, 25
Faith is weak
Joshua 1:6–9
Matthew 8:5–13
Luke 12:22–31
Hebrews 11
Far from God
Psalm 42:5–11
Psalm 139:1–18
Acts 17:22–30
Feeling inadequate
1 Corinthians 1:20–31
2 Corinthians 12:9, 10
Philippians 4:12, 13
Feeling strong
Psalm 18:32–35
Romans 12:3–16

Friends fail
Psalm 27:10–14
Psalm 41
Luke 17:3, 4
2 Timothy 4:16–18
Ill or in pain
Psalm 103:1–4
Leaving home
Psalm 121
Proverbs 3:1–7
Mark 10:28–30
Lonely
Psalm 23
John 14:15–21
Revelation 3:20
Needing guidance
Psalm 32:8–10
Psalm 37:3–7, 23, 24
Isaiah 30:19–21
John 16:12, 13
Needing peace
Isaiah 26:3,4
John 14:27
Romans 5:1–5
Philippians 4:4–7
Needing sleep
Psalm 4
Proverbs 3:13–26
1 Peter 5:7
2 Corinthians 12:9, 10
Praying
Luke 11:1–13
Luke 18:1–14
John 14:12–14
Sorrowful
Isaiah 53:1–6
Isaiah 61:1–3
2 Corinthians 1:3–11
Revelation 21:1–5
Successful
Deuteronomy 8:10–20
Tempted
Psalm 1
Matthew 4:1–10
1 Corinthians 10:12, 13
James l:12–15
Thankful
Psalm 92:1–5
Psalm 100
Ephesians 5:18–20
Troubled
Psalm 107:1–31
John 14:1–6
Wanting courage
John 3:16, 17
Acts 4:13–31
1 John 1:5–10
Ephesians 6:10–20
Weary
Psalm 116:5–14
Isaiah 40:28–31
Matthew 11:28–30
Luke 15:11–24